Herbert Puchta and Jeff Stranks

# English in Mind

## Second edition

## Workbook Starter

T0349653

CAMBRIDGE
UNIVERSITY PRESS

# Welcome section

## A

### 1 Say *Hello* and *Goodbye*

What are the words? Write them in the correct picture.

night   morning   evening   ~~afternoon~~

1  Good *afternoon*   | 2  Good _____ | 3  Good _____ | 4  Good _____

## B

### 1 International words

**a**  ► CD3 T2  Look at the pictures. Listen and write the numbers 1–12.

**b**  ► CD3 T2  Listen again and write the words. Then check with the list on page 6 of the Student's Book.

A

B

C  |7|

*taxi*

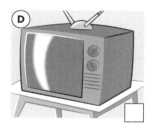

D

E

F

G

H

I

J

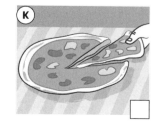

K

L

## 2 Classroom objects

What are the words? Write them in the picture.

pne    abdro    lepnic    tnokeoob    ~~wwdion~~    kdse    rchia    orod

1    window

3

2

4

7

5

6

8

## 3 Plural nouns

**a** Look at these examples for writing plurals.

| | |
|---|---|
| door | doors |
| phone | phones |
| hobby | hobbies |
| watch | watches |

**b** Complete the table.

| Singular | Plural |
|---|---|
| 1 hotel | hotels |
| 2 page | |
| 3 notebook | |
| 4 sandwich | |
| 5 city | |
| 6 taxi | |
| 7 nationality | |

**c** Write the numbers and the plural form of the words.

sandwich    child    woman    ~~computer~~    person    man

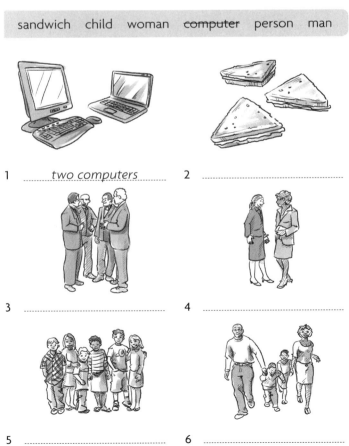

1    two computers    2

3    4

5    6

## C

### 1 Adjectives

Look at the pictures. If the adjective is correct, write (✔). If the adjective is wrong, write the correct adjective.

*small*
1 a ~~big~~ restaurant

2 an expensive pen ✔

3 a new computer

4 an interesting book

5 a bad football team

6 a big hamburger

7 an old taxi

8 a good hotel

### 2 a/an

Write *a* or *an*.

1 ___*a*___ good team
2 _____ small museum
3 _____ interesting book
4 _____ big television

5 _____ cheap pencil
6 _____ expensive hotel
7 _____ old city
8 _____ boring DVD

### 3 The alphabet

▶ CD3 T3 Listen to the spelling. Write the letters. What is the sentence?

*Lu*_____

▶ CD3 T4 Listen and write the words.

1 Name: Kevin _____
  City: _____

2 Name: Julie _____
  City: _____

### 4 Colours

Look at the pictures. Fill in the puzzle with the colours (1–6). What is the colour in number seven?

| ¹G | R | E | ⁷Y | | |
|---|---|---|---|---|---|
| | | ² | | | |
| | | ³ | | | |
| | | ⁴ | | | |
| ⁵ | | | | | |
| | | ⁶ | | | |

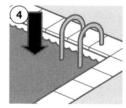
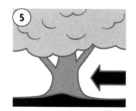

7 _____

## D

## 1 Asking and answering

▶ CD3 T5 Complete the dialogues with the words in the box. Then listen and check.

> can help   problem   Thank you   Excuse me
> ~~OK~~   What does this mean   I don't know
> don't understand

1   Kim:  The homework is on page 12. ____OK____ ?

   James:  Yes, great. [1]_____ , Kim.

2   Ben:  I [2]_____ these words.

   Mike:  No [3]_____ , Ben.

   I [4]_____ you!

   Ben:  Thanks, Mike!

3   Teacher:  What's the answer, Kate?

   Kate:  Sorry, Miss. [5]_____ !

4   Paul:  [6]_____ , Miss.

   Teacher:  Yes?

   Paul:  [7]_____ ? This word here,

   on page 28.

   Teacher:  Let me see.

## 2 Numbers 0-20

Write the answers.

1   nine + nine   = ____eighteen____

2   four + seven   = _____

3   two + twelve   = _____

4   one + eight   = _____

5   three + two   = _____

6   twelve + eight   = _____

7   ten + seven   = _____

8   four + eight   = _____

## 3 Numbers 20-100

**a** Write the next two numbers.

1   ten   thirty   fifty   ____seventy____   _____

2   four   eight   sixteen   _____   _____

3   forty-one   fifty-two   sixty-three   _____   _____

4   eighty-four   eighty-one   seventy-eight   _____   _____

5   twenty-nine   thirty-three   thirty-seven   _____   _____

**b**   ▶ CD3 T6 Listen and ⊙circle the numbers you hear.

1   ⑬   30

2   15   50

3   17   70

4   14   40

5   16   60

6   18   80

# 1 He's a footballer

## 1 Grammar

**✱ The verb be (singular)**

**a** Match the sentences in 1b with the pictures. Write numbers 1–7 in the boxes.

**b** Look at the underlined words. Write the short form, with 'm, 's or 're.

1 <u>It is</u> a boring film.

........It's........

2 <u>She is</u> an excellent singer.

........................................

3 <u>You are</u> a great teacher.

........................................

4 <u>It is</u> a new computer game.

........................................

5 <u>Richard is</u> from New York.

........................................

6 <u>Australia is</u> a big country.

........................................

7 <u>I am</u> Carla. <u>What is</u> your name?

.............................. ..............................

**c** Complete the dialogues.

1 A: Is Dinara Safina a film star?

B: No, _she's_ a tennis player.

2 A: Ashton Kutcher is an English actor, I think.

B: No, he isn't . ..............................
from the USA.

3 A: Is this DVD good?

B: Yes, .......................... great!

4 A: I think .......................... from Italy.

B: No, I'm not. I'm American.

5 A: What's *porta* in English?

B: .......................... 'door'.

A

B

C

D

Australia

UK

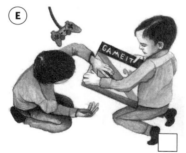
E

F

7

G

**d** Write the negative forms in the table.

| Positive | Negative – full forms | Negative – short forms |
|---|---|---|
| 1 I am | I am not | I'm not |
| 2 You are | | |
| 3 He is | | |
| 4 She is | | |
| 5 It is | | |

**e** Write positive or negative sentences.

1 he / a singer

*He isn't a singer.*

2 she / British

*She's British.*

3 it / Japanese

4 she / the winner

5 it / boring

6 you / a film star

7 it / expensive

8 you / a bad dog

**f** Put the words in order to make questions.

1 you / OK / Are

*Are you OK?*

2 British / she / Is

_____?

3 Istanbul / you / Are / from

_____?

4 right / I / Am

_____?

5 big / a / Is / it / city

_____?

6 Brad / Pitt / good / a / actor / Is

_____?

**9** ▶ **CD3 T7** Write questions. Then listen, check and repeat.

1 She's American.

*Is she American?*

2 You're from Japan.

_____

3 He's a good footballer.

_____

4 It's a cheap restaurant.

_____

5 I'm the winner!

_____

6 Broadway's in New York.

_____

7 The hotel's expensive.

_____

8 Maria's from Spain.

_____

9 You're a singer.

_____

10 The answer's on page 5.

_____

## 2 Vocabulary

### ✱ Countries

**a** Write the names of the countries on the map.

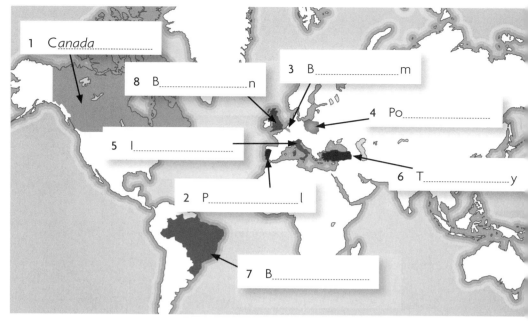

1 *Canada*

8 B_____n

3 B_____m

4 Po_____

5 I_____

6 T_____y

2 P_____l

7 B_____

### ✱ Nationalities

**b** Find seven nationalities in the word search.

| I | T | A | A | L | L | B | A | R | H | T |
|---|---|---|---|---|---|---|---|---|---|---|
| T | U | R | M | I | S | R | U | S | S | I |
| A | R | C | E | F | T | I | O | I | A | N |
| L | L | I | R | A | T | T | A | L | S | Q |
| I | D | P | I | S | W | I | S | S | T | B |
| A | H | O | C | W | I | S | T | P | V | E |
| N | S | L | A | A | S | H | R | A | I | L |
| I | P | I | N | S | T | A | G | L | O | G |
| A | U | S | T | R | A | L | I | A | N | I |
| N | X | H | T | U | R | K | I | S | H | A |
| A | M | E | X | T | R | S | P | F | E | N |

**d** **Vocabulary bank** Find the country names. Write them and add the nationalities.

1 ECFRNA      *France / French*

2 GETYP       _____

3 TIRGANENA   _____

4 HCEIL       _____

5 ERUP        _____

6 ROKEA       _____

7 OMBAICOL    _____

8 AAILTHND    _____

**c** Where are they from? Write two sentences about each person.

1 *He's from Brazil.*
  *He's Brazilian.*

2 _____

3 _____

4 _____

5 _____

6 _____

## 3 Pronunciation

▶ **CD3 T8** Listen and underline the word you hear.

1 Poland      <u>Polish</u>

2 Australia   Australian

3 Russia      Russian

4 Germany     German

5 Turkey      Turkish

6 Canada      Canadian

## 4 Grammar

★ *wh-* question words

**a** Match the questions and answers.

1 What's your name? ——— a He's OK.
2 Who's she? ——— b Kate.
3 How are you? c I'm fine, thanks.
4 How's Nick? d Mr Jones.
5 Where are you from? e I don't know.
6 Who's your English teacher? f Turkey.

**b** Complete the sentences. Use *Who, Where, What* or *How*.

1 I don't know her. ......*Who*...... is she?

2 ..................'s your phone number?

3 .................. are you from?

4 ..................'s the name of the hotel?

5 A: ..................'s Sydney?

   B: It's in Australia.

6 A: ..................'s that girl?

   B: My friend Sally.

7 .................. old is she?

8 A: ..................'s this?

   B: It's my vocabulary notebook.

## 5 Culture in mind

Look at the pictures and complete the sentences.

1 It's in
   ...*Australia*... .

2 He's ............................. .

3 .............................
   from Argentina.

4 It's a .............................
   city.

5 I'm ............................. .

6 She .............................
   in Germany.

## 6 Study help

★ Vocabulary

**a** For every unit, write new words in your Vocabulary notebook. Write them in groups. For example:

| Classroom things | Classroom verbs |
|---|---|
| *desk* | *listen* |
| *board* | *read* |
| *pen* | |
| | |
| | |
| | |
| | |

**b** Write these words in the lists.

> pencil  write  look at  chair  notebook
> say  ask  table  match

**c** Look at the words in Unit 1 of your Student's Book. Write all the words you can find in these lists. Don't forget to look in the Vocabulary bank too!

| Countries | Nationalities | Jobs |
|---|---|---|
| *Italy* | *Italian* | *film star* |
| *Spain* | | |
| *China* | | |
| | | |

# Skills in mind

## 7 Read

Read the text. Then write *T* (true) or *F* (false).

> I'm Helen. I'm fourteen and I'm British. My home is in Wells. It's an old city, but it isn't very big. My address is 32 Castle Road and my phone number is 01749 652013.
>
> My best friend is Michael. He's from Ireland and his father is French. Michael is fifteen, so he isn't in my class at school. He isn't a very good football player, but I think he's a great singer. He's a good friend and he helps me with my homework.

1   The girl's name is Helen.    ☐ *T*

2   She's from Britain.    ☐

3   Wells is a new city.    ☐

4   It's a small city.    ☐

5   Michael is Helen's friend.    ☐

6   He's from France.    ☐

7   He isn't in Helen's class.    ☐

8   He's an excellent footballer.    ☐

### READING TIP

*New words*

What happens if you don't know a word in a reading text?

- You can understand the text even if you don't know all the words.

- Look at the word. Is it similar to a word in your language?

- Look at the other words in the sentence, and think about the new word. Can you guess the meaning?

## 8 Write

Complete the interview with Helen. Write one word in each space.

**Interviewer:** Where ¹ ___*are*___ ² ___*you*___ from?

**Helen:** ³ _____ from ⁴ _____ . It's a city in England.

**Interviewer:** ⁵ _____ it a big city?

**Helen:** ⁶ _____ , it ⁷ _____ .

**Interviewer:** ⁸ _____ your ⁹ _____ ?

**Helen:** It's 32 Castle Road.

**Interviewer:** I know Michael's your ¹⁰ _____ friend. Is ¹¹ _____ Irish?

**Helen:** Yes, ¹² _____ ¹³ _____ .

**Interviewer:** ¹⁴ _____ old ¹⁵ _____ he?

**Helen:** ¹⁶ _____ ¹⁷ _____ .

# Unit check

## 1 Fill in the spaces

Complete the dialogues with the words in the box.

> Is   Polish   actor   from   Who's   teacher   ~~What's~~   is   Belgium   isn't

1   A:   Hello. ___*What's*___ your name?

B:   I'm Dieter and I'm from [1]_____ . This [2]_____ my friend Sonia.

A:   Is she [3]_____ Russia?

B:   No, she [4]_____ . She's [5]_____ .

2   A:   [6]_____ this?

B:   He's Luc Duval.

A:   [7]_____ he an [8]_____ ?

B:   No, he's a [9]_____ .

| | 9 |

## 2 Choose the correct answers

Circle the correct answer: a, b or c.

1   I think he's great! He's my _____ .

a (hero)   b singer   c winner

2   She's a famous film _____ .

a player   b actress   c model

3   Ricardo is _____ .

a Switzerland   b Spain   c Swiss

4   How old _____ ?

a she is   b she's   c is she

5   _____ is a big country.

a Canada   b French   c Russian

6   This tennis player _____ Australian.

a are   b aren't   c isn't

7   _____ are you from?

a What   b Where   c How

8   Is _____ a Japanese flag?

a he   b she   c it

9   _____ your address?

a What's   b Who's   c Where's

| | 8 |

## 3 Vocabulary

Underline the correct word in each sentence.

1   My friend lives in Tokyo. That's in *Japanese / Japan*.

2   Pedro speaks Spanish. He's *Colombia / Colombian*.

3   People in some parts of *Canadian / Canada* speak English and French.

4   I think *China / Chinese* is a difficult language.

5   She's from Brazil. She speaks *Portugal / Portuguese*.

6   I love going to Athens. *Greece / Greek* food is very good.

7   Is this the *Germany / German* flag?

8   *Irish / Ireland* is beautiful. It's very green.

9   She's from Bangkok. That's in *Thai / Thailand*.

| | 8 |

## How did you do?

Total:   | 25 |

|  | Very good<br>20 – 25 |  | OK<br>14 – 19 |  | Review Unit 1 again<br>0 – 13 |

# 2 We're a new band

## 1 Remember and check

Match the two parts of the sentences, and write the name of the speaker: *Kate, Matt, Chuck* or *AM* (audience member). Check with the dialogue on page 18 of the Student's Book.

| | | | |
|---|---|---|---|
| 1 | *Kate* | This is | a new band. |
| 2 | | We're a | b are you? |
| 3 | | Chuck and I | c our first song for you today. |
| 4 | | I'm | d the same city? |
| 5 | | How old | e are 19. |
| 6 | | Are you all from | f from Coventry. |

## 2 Grammar

✷ The verb *be*: plural, negatives and questions

**a** Look at the pictures and complete the sentences.

...*I'm*... a tennis player.

.................... my favourite singer.

I think .................... Australian.

What's this in English?
.................... a notebook.

.................... from Germany.

.................... the winners.

.................... fantastic!

.................... boring.

**b** Write true sentences with the verb *be*.

1 Avril Lavigne / American — Avril Lavigne *isn't American. She's Canadian.*

2 Fernando Alonso / racing driver — *Fernando Alonso is a racing driver.*

3 Tokyo / city in China

4 My favourite restaurant / expensive

5 I / British

6 Ferrari cars / cheap

7 Daniel Radcliffe / sports star

8 We / in Rome

**c** Match the questions and answers.

1 Is he German?
2 Are they a Brazilian band?
3 Is this CD expensive?
4 Are you and John footballers?
5 Are you from Poland?
6 Are Ann and Sophie good singers?
7 Am I a good tennis player?
8 Is she your friend?

a No, she isn't. I think she's boring.
b No, it isn't. It's quite cheap.
c Yes, I think you are.
d Yes, he is. He's from Hamburg.
e No, they aren't. They're from Spain.
f No, I'm not. I'm Russian.
g Yes, we are. We're in the school team.
h Yes, they are. They're great.

**d** Write the questions.

1 Maria / from Milan?
*Is Maria from Milan?*

2 Ken and Sandy / American?

3 I / a good singer?

4 Where / you from, Sarah?

5 the film / interesting?

6 you and Robert / football players?

7 James Blunt / popular in Belgium?

8 Julie and I / good actors?

9 Who / you?

10 What / your phone number?

**e** Read the questions and write true answers.

1 Are you a teacher?
*No, I'm not. I'm a student.*

2 Are you a good singer?

3 Are you from New York?

4 Are you and your friends in a band?

5 Are CDs expensive in your country?

6 Is your mother a tennis player?

7 Is your teacher British?

8 Is your school very big?

★ *I (don't) like ... / Do you like ... ?*

**f** Complete the dialogue.

Kate: Do __you like__ sports?

Ben: Yes, I [1]_____ , I [2]_____
football and [3]_____ . But I
[4]_____ volleyball.

Kate: [5]_____ you [6]_____
golf?

Ben: [7]_____ , I [8]_____ .
It's boring!

## 3 Vocabulary

**✱ Positive and negative adjectives**

**a** (Circle) the correct word.

1 I don't like pizza. I think it's *awful / wonderful*.
2 I like this DVD. It's *boring / fantastic*.
3 Justin Timberlake is my favourite singer. He's *terrible / great*.
4 I don't want to listen to The Verve. I think they're *wonderful / terrible*.

**b** Use the words in the box to write about the pictures.

| | | | |
|---|---|---|---|
| I like … | I think it's … | great | terrible |
| I really like … | I think they're … | awful | wonderful |
| I don't like … | | fantastic | |

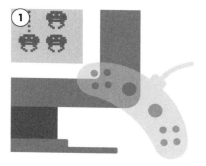

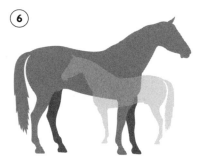

1 *I don't like computer games. I think they're boring.*
2 ..................................................................................
3 ..................................................................................
4 ..................................................................................
5 ..................................................................................
6 ..................................................................................

<u>Underline</u> the correct word.

1 I love Tony's restaurant. Their tomato soup is *disgusting / <u>delicious</u>*.
2 This film is *dreadful / brilliant*. I really don't like it.
3 He's a *useless / brilliant* footballer. He scores lots of goals.
4 This room is *disgusting / excellent*. Let's go to a different hotel.
5 He's good on the guitar, but as a singer he's *useless / delicious*.
6 Read this book! It's *excellent / useless*.

## 4 Grammar

**✱ Object pronouns**

Complete the sentences with object pronouns.

1 I don't like ..... *her* ..... . She isn't very interesting.
2 Paul's a good singer. Listen to ................................. .
3 Dogs are great. I like ................................. a lot.
4 Bye! See ................................. on Friday!
5 Look! A picture of my favourite band! I want ................................. !
6 I like James, but he doesn't like ................................. .

## 5 Pronunciation

✱ /ɪ/ and /iː/

**a** ▶ **CD3 T9** Listen to the underlined sounds. Write the words in the lists. Then listen again, check and repeat.

see  think  singer  please
film  read  museum  cinema
CD  big  people  women

| /ɪ/ is | /iː/ three |
|---|---|
| think | see |
| | |
| | |
| | |
| | |
| | |

**b** ▶ **CD3 T10** Listen and repeat.

1 Three big museums.
2 We think he's Swiss.
3 Fifteen CDs, please.
4 The Italian singer is the winner.

## 6 Everyday English

Complete the dialogues with the words in the box.

Cool!  Of course!  I'm sorry  I know

1 A: Do you like this song?
   B: _____ It's great!

2 A: Here – have an ice cream!
   B: Oh, _____ Paula – I don't like ice cream.

3 A: Look! I've got the new Kings of Leon CD.
   B: _____ Let's listen to it now!

4 A: It's Saturday tomorrow!
   B: _____ ! No school. Cool!

## 7 Study help

✱ Pronunciation

Mark the stress on new words in your Vocabulary notebook like this:

● underline the stressed sound
   fantastic  wonderful  favourite

● use the sign '. This is the sign in a dictionary.
   fan'tastic  'wonderful  'favourite

**a** Write the sign ' to show the stress in these words.

1 popular
2 American
3 Japanese
4 terrible
5 computer
6 concert
7 seventeen

**b** Write adjectives from Unit 2 in this list. Mark the stress.

fan'tastic  _____
_____  _____
_____  _____

# Skills in mind

## 8 Read and listen

**a** ▶CD3 T11 Look at this girl's internet homepage. Listen and complete the text. Write one word in each space.

> # Hi! Welcome to my homepage.
>
> My name is **Judy Dahrendorf.** I live in Santa Cruz in California and I really like rock [1] _music_ . Can you guess who my [2] _____ rock stars are? Yes, you're right: **they're the 'Kings of Leon'!**
>
> Here are **four things** I want to tell you about them:
>
> * There are four people in the [3] _____ : – three brothers and a cousin! They are **Caleb, Nathan, Jared** and **Matthew Followill.**
>
> * My favourite King of Leon [4] _____ Caleb. I think he's [5] _____ ! And he's a [6] _____ singer!
>
> * My favourite Kings of Leon song is *Closer*. All my friends say their favourite is *Use Somebody*. (I think it's [7] _____ good, but it isn't my favourite.)
>
> * The Kings of Leon are all [8] _____ . Matthew is from Mississippi, and the other three are [9] _____ Tennessee.
>
> Do you [10] _____ my homepage? I hope so. And I hope you like KOL, too!

---

### LISTENING TIP

*Before you listen*

* Look at the pictures with the text. What is the topic of the text?
* Read the text before you listen.
* Try to guess the missing words. Write your ideas in pencil in the text.
* What <u>type</u> of word is it? Is it the name of a thing or a person? Is it a verb (*is / are / go / like / listen* ...)? Is it an adjective (*popular / cheap / wonderful* ...)?

**b** Read the text again. Write *T* (true) or *F* (false).

1 Judy is Australian. `F`
2 The Kings of Leon are Judy's favourite band. ☐
3 There are five people in the band. ☐
4 Judy really likes the song *Closer*. ☐
5 Judy thinks *Use Somebody* is a terrible song. ☐
6 The Kings of Leon are all from Mississippi. ☐

# Unit check

## 1 Fill in the spaces

Complete the sentences with the words in the box.

> wonderful   are   she's   together   ~~band~~   aren't   we're   from   them   film

Mick, Keith and Carla are in a _____band_____ . Carla's [1]_____ Australia and [2]_____ the singer.
The other two [3]_____ from Canada. People don't know [4]_____ in my country, so they
[5]_____ very popular here. But I think their music is [6]_____ . They're in a new [7]_____
now. My friend Elizabeth and I want to see it [8]_____ , and [9]_____ really excited.  | 9 |

## 2 Choose the correct answers

(Circle) the correct answer: a, b or c.

1   Cathy's really _____ about the concert.

   a fantastic   b popular   c (excited)

2   A:  I want a sandwich. _____

   B:  No, thanks. I'm OK.

   a Guess what?   b What about you?   c Let's go.

3   We don't like this CD. It's _____ .

   a favourite   b awful   c wonderful

4   Jan and Petra _____ from Germany.

   a is   b isn't   c aren't

5   A:  Is she a good singer?   B:  Yes, we really like _____ .

   a us   b her   c him

6   _____ Brazilian?

   a You are   b Are you   c Do you

7   Paris _____ the capital of Italy.

   a not   b isn't   c aren't

8   A:  Do you like classical music?

   B:  Yes, I _____ .

   a do   b is   c am

9   Listen to the words and repeat _____ .

   a it   b him   c them   | 8 |

## 3 Vocabulary

Find the adjectives. Complete the sentences.

1   Thanks for the present. It's _____great_____ (agrte).

2   Have a piece of this cake. It's _____ (odcielsiu).

3   She is a _____ (lliirnatb) story teller. Let's go and listen to her.

4   Look, there are lots of mice in the kitchen. It's _____ (dgigsutnis).

5   Don't ask me for help with French. My French is _____ (elessus).

6   I don't want to hear this song again! It's _____ (dfldreau).

7   I don't like this computer. It's _____ (rltebrie).

8   Thank you for the book. It's _____ (xteelnecl).

9   My favourite rock band is Arctic Monkeys. They're _____ (nattiasfc).   | 8 |

## How did you do?

Total: | 25 |

| ☺ | Very good 20 – 25 | ☺ | OK 14 – 19 | ☹ | Review Unit 2 again 0 – 13 |

# 3 She lives in Washington

## 1 Remember and check

Match the two parts of the sentences. Then check with the text on page 26 of the Student's Book.

1 Michelle Obama          a the White House in Washington.
2 Millions of people see   b important projects for the American people.
3 She lives in            c very busy.
4 She's                   d is American.
5 She works on            e her husband with his work.
6 She also helps          f her on TV.

## 2 Grammar

**✳ Present simple: positive and negative**

**a** Find 11 more verbs in the word snake. Write them under the pictures.

learnreadworkliveplayspeakstopwatchwritestudyunderstandlisten

_____

*learn*

**b** Complete the sentences with the verb + *s*, *es* or *ies*.

1 She _____*likes*_____ the film. (like)

2 James _____ TV after school. (watch)

3 Sarah _____ to the cinema on Saturdays. (go)

4 He _____ German. (speak)

5 My father _____ to classical music. (listen)

6 School _____ at 3.30. (finish)

7 My friend _____ in a shop. (work)

8 Lisa _____ Music at school. (study)

**c** Complete the sentences. Use the correct form of the verbs in the box.

> speak   watch   ~~listen~~   understand   write   live   play

1   I _____listen_____ to pop music on the radio.
2   J.K. Rowling _____ books about Harry Potter.
3   My cousins _____ a lot of films.
4   We _____ volleyball at school.
5   My aunt _____ four languages.
6   You _____ in a big house!
7   I _____ the question, but I don't know the answer.

**d** Look at the pictures and write sentences.

1   Caroline / speak
    *Caroline speaks Spanish but she doesn't speak French.*
2   We / play _____
    _____
3   Sam / like _____
4   Julie / listen _____
    _____
5   Tony and Jill / watch _____
    _____

✱ **Present simple: questions and short answers**

**e** Complete the questions with *Do* or *Does*.

1   _Do_ you like sport?
2   _____ Marcel live in Paris?
3   _____ your mother listen to music?
4   _____ Peter and Jack sometimes go to the cinema?
5   _____ you play computer games at home?
6   _____ we know the answer to this question?
7   _____ your uncle use a mobile phone?

**f** Write the questions. Then write true answers.

1   you / watch TV before school?
    *Do you watch TV before school?*
    *Yes, I do.* or *No, I don't.*
2   you / always finish your homework?
    _____
    _____
3   your best friend / like football?
    _____
    _____
4   you and your friends / play volleyball?
    _____
    _____
5   your teacher / speak English?
    _____
    _____
6   your friends / understand Russian?
    _____
    _____

# 3 Pronunciation

✱ /s/, /z/ and /ɪz/

▶ **CD3 T12**  Listen and write the underlined sound: /s/, /z/ or /ɪz/. Then listen again, check and repeat.

1  She likes it here.  ___/s/___

2  Does Anna learn music?  ...........

3  Sam watches films.  ...........

4  She writes a lot of letters.  ...........

5  He lives in London.  ...........

6  The class finishes soon.  ...........

7  Paul speaks Italian.  ...........

# 4 Vocabulary and grammar

✱ Family and possessive 's

**a**  Look at the family tree and complete the sentences.

1  Rosa is Maria's ___mother___ .

2  Barbara is Maria's ........................... .

3  Maria's ........................... are Steve and John.

4  Steve's ........................... is Patricia.

5  Rosa is Barbara's ........................... .

6  David is ........................... uncle.

7  Sally's ........................... are Maria's grandparents.

8  Matt is ........................... father.

9  ........................... sister is Sally.

Patricia + Martin

Matt + Sally    David + Rosa

Barbara    Steve    Maria    John

**b**  Draw your family tree. Write the family words and the people's names.

**c**  Write five sentences about your family.

*My father's name is David and my mother's name is Rosa.*
*Steve and John are my brothers and Barbara is ...*

................................................................................

................................................................................

................................................................................

................................................................................

................................................................................

**d** **Vocabulary bank** Complete the sentences with the correct words.

1 My mother's mother is my father's ........................... .

2 My name's Paul. I'm my grandpa's ........................... .

3 My name is Marianne. I'm my grandpa's ........................... .

4 Paul and Marianne are their grandpa and grandma's ........................... .

5 My grandma and my grandpa are my ........................... .

6 My brother Tony's wife is Janet. Her father is Tony's ........................... .

## 5 Grammar

✱ Possessive adjectives

Underline the correct words.

1 I play games on *my / I / me* computer.

2 No problem! We can help you with *you / your / our* homework.

3 Dave lives in England, but *his / her / their* grandparents live in France.

4 Amy watches *he / she / her* favourite football team on TV.

5 My friends and I like *me / their / our* new teacher.

6 The classroom is big, but *its / his / their* windows are small.

7 My aunt and uncle go shopping in town, but *his / her / their* children don't go.

## 6 Culture in mind

What are the words? Write them under the pictures. Then check with the text on page 30 of the Student's Book.

souhe   yceorgr soph   ltfa   saetcrrye   etleaevbsg   uirft

① ........................... *fruit* ...........................

② ***Grocery shop*** ...........................

③ ...........................

④ ...........................

⑤ ...........................

⑥ ...........................

## 7 Study help

✱ Vocabulary

**a** In your Vocabulary notebook, write words together. For example:

**go**   to the cinema
       for a walk
       shopping

**speak**   a language
          French
          to my friend

**b** Write words that go with these verbs.

Verbs

work   *in a shop*          write   ...........................

       ...........................          ...........................

play   ...........................          read   ...........................

       ...........................          ...........................

watch   ...........................          listen to   ...........................

       ...........................          ...........................

## 8 Listen

▶ **CD3 T13** Listen to Alice talking about her friend Rebecca. Write ✔ or ✘ in the boxes.

Alice    Rebecca

① London ✔

② family ☐

③ ☐

④ ☐

⑤ ☐

⑥ ☐

⑦ ☐

## 9 Write

Write sentences about Mateo.

*Mateo is 15. He lives in Rome.*

_____

_____

_____

_____

_____

### WRITING TIP

Don't always repeat names in your writing – use pronouns. For example:

                He
*Mateo is 15. ~~Mateo~~ lives in Rome.*

                              his
*Mateo's sister is Sonia and ~~Mateo's~~ brother is …*

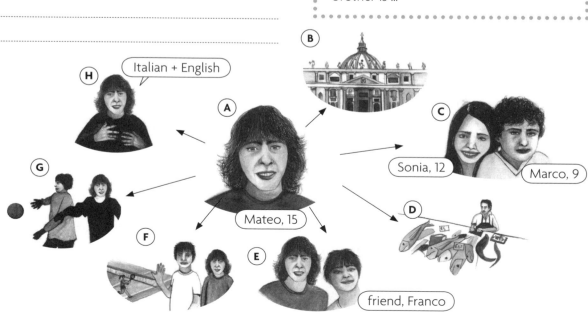

H — Italian + English

A — Mateo, 15

B

C — Sonia, 12    Marco, 9

D

E

F

G

friend, Franco

# Unit check

## 1 Fill in the spaces

Complete the sentences with the words in the box.

| learn | doesn't | have | live | ~~her~~ | their | volleyball | don't | Tara's | speaks |

Alison Short and _____*her*_____ sister Tara [1]_____ in Cambridge with [2]_____ parents. Mr Short [3]_____ work, but Mrs Short is a teacher at [4]_____ school. The two sisters [5]_____ music, and Alison [6]_____ French and Italian. They play [7]_____ together, but they [8]_____ fights because they [9]_____ like the same music.

☐ 9

## 2 Choose the correct answers

(Circle) the correct answer: a, b or c.

1  I've got five brothers and _____ .

   a (sisters)  b grandmothers  c fathers

2  Your mother's brother is your _____ .

   a cousin  b uncle  c aunt

3  Dave goes for a walk with _____ dog.

   a he  b his  c him

4  We have 28 people in _____ class.

   a our  b their  c my

5  My cousins _____ football.

   a like  b likes  c do like

6  Maria _____ in Portugal.

   a live  b lives  c don't live

7  _____ speak English?

   a You are  b Are you  c Do you

8  A:  Do they work in this town?

   B:  No, _____ .

   a they aren't  b they do  c they don't

9  Does _____ cartoons on TV?

   a she watches  b you watch  c Peter watch

☐ 8

## 3 Vocabulary

Complete the sentences with family words.

1  I've got an uncle called Jim. His son is my _____*cousin*_____ Alex.

2  Karen's grandma is Sally. Sally's husband died, so Karen hasn't got a _____ .

3  Michelle Obama's _____ is the President of the USA. Michelle is his _____ .

4  Michelle Obama's father is dead, so the President hasn't got a _____ .

5  Jane and Tony love their grandparents, and their grandparents love Jane and Tony, their _____ .

6  Kate and Tom are married. Kate's brother Nick is Tom's _____ . Tom's mother is Kate's _____ , and his sister is Kate's _____ .

☐ 8

## How did you do?

Total: ☐ 25

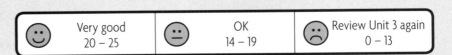

| ☺ | Very good 20 – 25 | ☺ | OK 14 – 19 | ☹ | Review Unit 3 again 0 – 13 |

# 4 Where's the café?

## 1 Remember and check

Look at the pictures. Fill in the crossword. Check with the text on page 32 of the Student's Book.

museum

open-top _____ → _____

Crossword:

1 Across: M U S E U M
2 Down: M
3
4
5
6

## 2 Vocabulary

**✴ Numbers 100 +**

**a** ▶ CD3 T14 Listen and circle the numbers you hear.

| 1 | (139) | 193 |
|---|-------|-----|
| 2 | 318 | 380 |
| 3 | 561 | 651 |
| 4 | 807 | 870 |
| 5 | 740 | 714 |
| 6 | 1,000 | 10,000 |
| 7 | 2,924 | 2,524 |

**b** ▶ CD3 T15 Listen and write the numbers you hear. Then write the answers in words.

1  12  +  _30_  =  _forty-two_

2  50  +  ____  =  ____

3  11  +  ____  =  ____

4  110 +  ____  =  ____

5  266 +  ____  =  ____

6  309 +  ____  =  ____

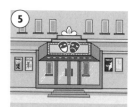

↓ _____ → _____

↓ bus _____   modern _____

## 3 Pronunciation

**✴ /ð/ and /θ/**

▶ CD3 T16 Listen to the sentences. Are the *th* sounds /θ/ (*three*) or /ð/ (*mother*)? Tick (✔) the correct box. Then listen again, check and repeat.

|   | /ð/ | /θ/ |
|---|-----|-----|
| 1 I think he's thirty. | ☐ | ☐ |
| 2 That's their father. | ☐ | ☐ |
| 3 They buy clothes together. | ☐ | ☐ |
| 4 Thanks for the birthday party. | ☐ | ☐ |

## 4 Grammar

**✱** *There's / there are*

**a** Complete the sentences with *'s* or *are*.

1 There *'s* _____ a good restaurant in this town.

2 There _____ over nine million people in London.

3 There _____ interesting clothes in this shop.

4 In London there _____ a river called the Thames.

5 There _____ an expensive cinema in the city centre.

6 There _____ six children in their family.

**b** Look at the picture and complete the text. Use *there's*, *there isn't*, *there are* or *there aren't*.

*There are* _____ only about 3,000 people in my town. It's very small, so ¹_____ a lot to do. ²_____ about 12 shops and ³_____ a good market here on Fridays, but ⁴_____ any supermarkets. ⁵_____ a cinema but that's OK – ⁶_____ a good collection of DVDs at the video shop. ⁷_____ two schools in the town and ⁸_____ an excellent restaurant called the Black Horse. ⁹_____ any trains here because ¹⁰_____ a station.

## 5 Vocabulary

**✱** *Places in towns*

**a** Match the words with the pictures. Write 1–8 in the boxes.

1 ~~library~~
2 bank
3 railway station
4 supermarket
5 newsagent
6 chemist
7 bookshop
8 post office

**b** **Vocabulary bank** Complete the sentences with the words from the box.

> police station  primary  ~~secondary~~  leisure centre  shopping centre  car park

1  Her children are 13 and 14. They go to ___secondary___ school.

2  My sister is six. She goes to _____ school.

3  Where is the big _____ _____ ? We want to buy lots of different things.

4  The _____ _____ is full. Where can we park the car?

5  There is a big _____ _____ in my town. You can swim, play squash, and do many other things there.

6  Look! An accident. Can you tell me where the _____ _____ is?

**c** Write the questions. Use *Is there a* or *Are there any*. Then write true answers.

1  good cafés / in your town?

   *Are there any good cafés in your town?*

   *Yes, there are.* or *No, there aren't.*

2  big post office / in your town?

   _____

   _____

3  bookshops / near your school?

   _____

   _____

4  good library / in your school?

   _____

   _____

5  railway station / near your home?

   _____

   _____

6  newsagents / in your street?

   _____

   _____

# 6 Grammar

## ✱ Positive imperatives

Write the sentences from the box under the pictures.

> Turn left.  Turn right.  Go home.
> Sit down.  ~~Listen to me.~~  Look!

1  ___Listen to me.___   2  _____

3  _____   4  _____

5  _____   6  _____

# 7 Vocabulary

## ✱ Directions

**a** Look at the pictures and complete the sentences.

**1** Café, Bookshop
**2** Park, Post Office
**3** Library, Supermarket, Chemist
**4** Newsagent, Restaurant, Bank

1  The café is ___next to the bookshop.___

2  The park is _____ .

3  The supermarket is _____ .

   The chemist is _____ .

4  The restaurant is _____ the _____

   and the _____ .

**b** Where does the tourist want to go? Look at the map and complete the dialogue. Start at the station.

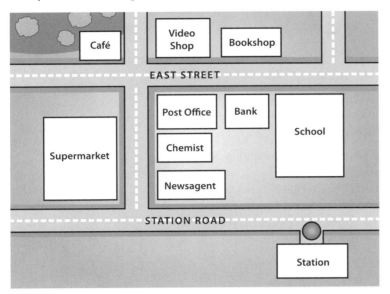

Tourist: Excuse me, where's the ¹_____ , please?

Woman: Go down Station Road and turn right. The ²_____ is on the right between the post office and the newsagent.

Tourist: Thanks. And is there a ³_____ near here?

Woman: Yes, there is. Turn right into East Street. The ⁴_____ is on the left opposite the bank.

Tourist: Thank you very much.

**c** Look at the map again. Give directions from the school to the café.

Tourist: Excuse me, is there a café near here?

You: Yes, ¹_____ Go ²_____ and turn ³_____ . The café is ⁴_____ .

## 8 Everyday English

Complete the dialogue with the phrases in the box.

> Wait a minute.   Really   I have no idea.   actually

A: See that boy? He's new at school. What's his name?

B: ¹_____

A: OK. Let's go and ask him.

B: Hello. What's your name?

C: Pedro. Pedro Aguilar.

B: Pedro? Oh, you're Spanish.

C: Well, ²_____ , I'm not Spanish. I'm from Colombia.

A: ³_____ ? That's interesting.

B: Yes, very interesting. ⁴_____ There's a girl in 3A called Angela. I think she's Colombian too.

C: Yes, she is. I know her very well.

## 9 Study help

★ Vocabulary

Sometimes it's a good idea to draw pictures or diagrams in your Vocabulary notebook. Draw pictures to show the meaning of these prepositions:

> ~~on~~   in   behind
> opposite   between
> near   next to   under

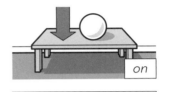

# Skills in mind

## 10 Read

**a** Read the text and complete the table.

Paul lives in a town called Katoomba in Australia. It's in the Blue Mountains, 110 km from Sydney, and there are about 18,000 people in the town.

There isn't a museum in Katoomba, but there's a library and an excellent cinema called The Edge. There are also lots of shops. Paul's parents often go shopping at the Coles supermarket and they buy their newspapers at Dixon's. Paul likes bicycles, and his favourite shop is Cycletech. His brother George sells books at a bookshop called Elizabeth's. Paul goes to Katoomba High School and his little sister goes to Katoomba North Public School.

Katoomba is very popular with tourists, so there are lots of hotels in the town. Tourists often come from Sydney by train – the trip takes two hours.

| Name | Type of business/shop |
|------|----------------------|
| 1 The Edge | *cinema* |
| 2 Coles | .......................... |
| 3 .......................... | newsagent |
| 4 .......................... | bicycle shop |
| 5 Elizabeth's | .......................... |

**b** Read the text again and answer the questions. Write short answers.

1 Is Sydney very near Katoomba?

   *No, it isn't.* .........................................

2 Are there twenty thousand people in Katoomba?

   ....................................................................

3 Do people watch films at The Edge?

   ....................................................................

4 Is there a museum in the town?

   ....................................................................

5 Do people buy clothes at Elizabeth's?

   ....................................................................

6 Is Paul's sister a student at his school?

   ....................................................................

7 Are there lots of tourists in Katoomba?

   ....................................................................

8 Is there a railway station in the town?

   ....................................................................

## 11 Write

Write a short text about a town that you like in your country or in a different country. Think about these questions.

- Is there a river / a beach?
- Is there a cinema? Are there any cafés and restaurants? Is there a station?
- What shops are there?
- What's your favourite place in town?

# Unit check

## 1 Fill in the spaces

Complete the sentences with the words in the box.

| opposite | there's | ~~centre~~ | market | are | takes | newsagent | aren't | train | between |

Martin lives in the city _____centre_____ and there ¹_____ lots of shops in his street. His house is
²_____ a chemist and a ³_____ . There's a ⁴_____ station ⁵_____ the house
and Martin ⁶_____ the train to school. There ⁷_____ any big supermarkets, but that's
no problem – ⁸_____ a very good ⁹_____ in the street every day.

| 9 |

## 2 Choose the correct answers

(Circle) the correct answer: a, b or c.

1 Change your money at the _____ .

  a (bank)  b market  c university

2 You can buy magazines at a _____ .

  a library  b chemist  c newsagent

3 100,000 = _____ .

  a a million  b a thousand hundred

  c a hundred thousand

4 The post office is _____ the corner.

  a on  b in  c in front

5 I want to send a _____ .

  a railway  b train  c letter

6 Go straight on and _____ left.

  a start  b turn  c send

7 I think there's _____ river in this town.

  a any  b a  c the

8 There _____ any good clothes in this shop.

  a are  b aren't  c isn't

9 A: Is the railway station near here?    B: _____

  a I have no idea.  b You're welcome.  c No, there isn't

| 8 |

## 3 Vocabulary

Find seven more names for places in town in the wordsnake. (There are three other words
which are not about places in towns.) Write the words on the lines below.

1 _____bus station_____

2 _____

3 _____

4 _____

5 _____

6 _____

7 _____

8 _____

| 7 |

## How did you do?

Total: | 24 |

| 😊 | Very good 20 – 24 | 😐 | OK 13 – 19 | 😟 | Review Unit 4 again 0 – 12 |

# 5 They've got brown eyes

## 1 Remember and check

Think about Sally the chimpanzee and underline the correct words. Then check with the text on page 40 of the Student's Book.

1 Sally is <u>four</u> / fourteen years old.
2 She's got blue / brown eyes.
3 She's got / She hasn't got a big family.
4 She likes / doesn't like bananas.
5 She lives in a park / forest.
6 She isn't intelligent / stupid.

## 2 Grammar

### ✱ Why ...? Because ...

a Match the questions and answers.

1 Why do people like football?
2 Why isn't the library open?
3 Why do you like these shoes?
4 Why are you happy today?

a Because it's my birthday.
b Because they're fashionable.
c Because it's an exciting game.
d Because it's Sunday today.

### ✱ has / have got

b Complete the sentences with has / have got. Use short forms where possible.

1 You __'ve got__ a fantastic DVD player!
2 Mr and Mrs Martin _____ a house near the river.
3 Sue _____ a new bicycle.
4 I _____ a very big family.
5 We _____ an excellent computer at home.
6 This town _____ two cinemas and a museum.
7 My brother _____ an interesting collection of stamps.
8 Chimpanzees _____ four fingers on each hand.

c Look at the table and write sentences about Jessie and her brother Tom. Use the correct form of have got.

|  | Jessie | Tom |
| --- | --- | --- |
| a bicycle | ✗ | ✔ |
| a mobile phone | ✔ | ✗ |
| a big family | ✗ | ✗ |
| a CD player | ✗ | ✔ |
| brown hair | ✔ | ✗ |
| brown eyes | ✔ | ✔ |
| a computer | ✔ | ✗ |

1 Jessie / bicycle _Jessie hasn't got a bicycle._
2 Tom / mobile phone _____
3 Jessie and Tom / big family _____
4 Tom / CD player _____
5 Jessie / brown hair _____
6 Jessie and Tom / brown eyes _____
7 Tom / computer _____
8 Jessie / computer _____

**d** Complete the questions. Then look at the pictures and write short answers.

1 A: _Have_ you _got_ a bicycle?

 B: _Yes, I have._

2 A: _____ Andy _____ a computer?

 B: _____ .

3 A: _____ you _____ a DVD player?

 B: _____ .

4 A: _____ Jane _____ a big nose?

 B: _____ .

5 A: _____ your parents _____ a car?

 B: _____ .

6 A: _____ Steve _____ a big family?

 B: _____ .

**e** Write four true sentences with the correct form of *have got* (positive or negative). Choose words from box A and box B.

| A | B |
|---|---|
| I   My parents   My sister   ~~My best friend~~<br>My friends   My English teacher   My aunt | an old car   brown hair   a nice smile<br>blue eyes   long fingers   ~~fashionable clothes~~ |

_My best friend has got fashionable clothes._

_____

_____   _____

## 3 Vocabulary
### ✱ Parts of the body

**a** Find 11 more parts of the body in the puzzle. Write the words under the pictures.

| L | A | G | X | T | O | T | (A | R | M) |
|---|---|---|---|---|---|---|---|---|---|
| A | E | Y | E | A | L | H | H | O | O |
| S | R | H | A | N | D | A | T | S | U |
| D | X | O | Q | Y | I | F | O | O | T |
| V | H | A | I | R | G | A | T | M | H |
| L | Y | N | X | M | W | C | H | E | H |
| E | A | F | N | O | S | E | U | A | B |
| G | R | A | F | K | G | C | M | R | V |
| F | I | N | G | E | R | D | B | Y | A |

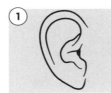
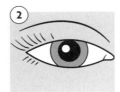
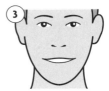

_____   _____   _____

_____   _____   _____

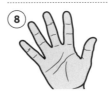
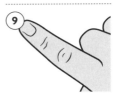

_____ _arm_   _____   _____

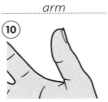
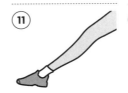
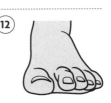

_____   _____   _____

**b** **Vocabulary bank** Look at the picture and write the words.

1   *eyebrow*

2   _____

3   _____

4   _____

5   _____

✱ Describing people

**c** Complete the descriptions with the words in the box. Then draw the two people's faces.

green   nose   wavy   ~~blonde~~   good-looking   smile   eyes

Janet has got straight ¹___*blonde*___ hair
and blue ²_____ . She's got a small
³_____ and a happy ⁴_____ .

I think Chris is very ⁵_____ . He's
got a long straight nose and his eyes are
⁶_____ . He's got ⁷_____
black hair.

✱ Giving personal information

**d** Match the questions and answers.

1   What's your surname?              a   C-L-A-R-K.

2   How do you spell that, please?    b   Yes, I have. It's 07976 648712.

3   What's your first name?           c   I'm 15.

4   How old are you?                  d   Clark.

5   What's your address?              e   01367 995024.

6   What's your telephone number?     f   Diana.

7   Have you got a mobile number?     g   16 Felton Street, Dover.

**e** ▶ **CD3 T17** Listen to the questions and reply with true information.

## 4 Pronunciation

**✳** /v/ *they've*

**▶CD3 T18** Listen and repeat.

1　They've got wavy hair.
2　We've got twelve TVs.
3　Steve lives near the river.
4　He gives five interviews every day.
5　Vivien drives to the university.

## 5 Culture in mind

Look at the pictures and write the names
of the pets.

> cat　hamster　~~dog~~　spider　lizard
> snake　rabbit　budgie　guinea pig

1 ..........dog..........

2 ....................

3 ....................

4 ....................

5 ....................

6 ....................

7 ....................

8 ....................

9 ....................

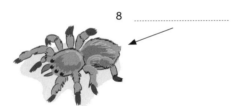

## 6 Study help

**✳** Vocabulary

**a**　In your Vocabulary notebook, write adjectives with their opposites. For example:

big　　　small
awful　　wonderful

**b**　Find opposites in the box and write them together in the lists.

> interesting　~~long~~　cheap　intelligent　curly　dark
> boring　straight　stupid　fair　expensive　~~short~~

Adjectives for hair　　　　　　　Other adjectives

......*long*......　......*short*......　....................　....................

....................　....................　....................　....................

....................　....................　....................　....................

# Skills in mind

## 7 Listen

▶ CD3 T19 Joe is talking about his sister's boyfriend. Listen and write the information in the table.

| | |
|---|---|
| 1 First name: | *Gilles* |
| 2 Nationality: | |
| 3 City: | *Geneva* |
| 4 Language: | |
| 5 Age: | |
| 6 Colour of eyes: | |
| 7 Colour of hair: | |

### LISTENING TIP

Listen to the spelling of *Gilles* in the recording. The speaker says 'double L', like this:

G - I - **double-L** - E - S

It's the same with telephone numbers.

For example: 0188 35669: oh one **double-eight**, three five **double-six** nine.

## 8 Read

**a** Read the letter. Which picture shows David and his family?

Dear Pietro

I'm David Ling, and I'm your new penfriend. I'm 15 and I live in Vancouver, a city in Canada. I've got short black hair and brown eyes.

My mother and father are from Hong Kong and we speak English and Chinese at home. My father works in a bank in the city centre and my mother works in a restaurant. My sister doesn't live at home, because she's got a job in a library in San Francisco. She's 22. My brother Jack is at university in Vancouver and he studies Computer Science.

Please write and tell me about you and your family.

All the best,

David

**b** Correct these sentences.

1 David's fourteen. *No, he isn't. He's fifteen.*

2 He's got long hair. _____

3 His parents are from Canada. _____

4 His mother hasn't got a job. _____

5 His sister lives in a library. _____

6 Jack works in a computer shop. _____

# Unit check

## 1 Fill in the spaces

Complete the sentences with the words in the box.

| clothes   eyes   fair   ~~are~~   wears   he's   isn't   haven't   good-looking   wavy |

Paul and Harry _____are_____ my brothers. Harry looks like Dad. He [1]_____ very tall and [2]_____ got blond [3]_____ hair. He wears dark [4]_____ and he thinks he's very [5]_____. Paul and I are also quite short, but we [6]_____ got [7]_____ hair – our hair is brown. We've got blue [8]_____ and Paul [9]_____ glasses. ▢ **9**

## 2 Choose the correct answers

(Circle) the correct answer: a, b or c.

1  You've got long arms and _____ .

   a foot  b mouths  c (legs)

2  Julie's eyes are _____ .

   a brown  b blond  c pink

3  I think your brother's very _____ .

   a curly  b wavy  c good-looking

4  She's got short _____ hair.

   a long  b straight  c medium-length

5  Rabbits have got big _____ .

   a nose  b ears  c faces

6  My first name is Helen and my _____ is Johnson.

   a surname  b age  c address

7  A lot of people _____ pets at home.

   a got  b have got  c has got

8  A:  Has Denise got a mobile phone?

   B:  Yes, she _____ .

   a got  b has  c does

9  Alan _____ glasses.

   a doesn't get  b doesn't got  c hasn't got ▨ **8**

## 3 Vocabulary

What are the words? Write the parts of the body.

1  eken        _____knee_____

2  twsri      _____

3  keche    _____

4  psli        _____

5  aerbloe   _____

6  kcen      _____

7  wbleo    _____

8  weebyor  _____

9  kbca      _____ ▨ **8**

## How did you do?

Total: ▢ **25**

| :) Very good 20 – 25 | :| OK 14 – 19 | :( Review Unit 5 again 0 – 13 |

## 1 Remember and check

Match the two parts of the words, and then write the words under the pictures.

| 1 | raw | cken |
|---|-----|------|
| 2 | mi | fly |
| 3 | su | ake |
| 4 | chi | ce |
| 5 | sn | shi |
| 6 | dragon | egg |

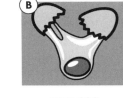

----------------

_raw egg_

----------------

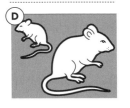

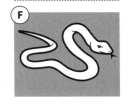

----------------

## 2 Vocabulary

**★ Food**

**a** ▶CD3 T20  Listen and write the numbers 1–14.

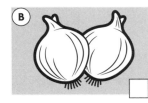

1

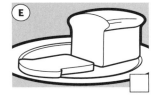

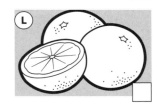

**b** Look at the pictures again. Write the names of the things in the table. Give the other two lists a heading.

| | | Meat | Groceries |
|---|---|------|-----------|
| _bananas_ | _onions_ | | _sugar_ |
| | | | |
| | | | |
| | | | |
| | | | |

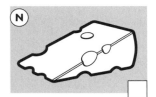

**c** **Vocabulary bank** Underline the word that is different from the others.

1  salt           pepper         <u>chocolate</u>      4  banana         yoghurt        apple
2  chocolate      ice cream      cereal             5  onion          cheese         garlic
3  beans          mushrooms      steak

# 3 Grammar

**✱ Countable and uncountable nouns**

**a** Write the words in the correct lists.

> banana̶   ri̶ce̶   onion   carrot   cheese
> salt   apple   sugar

Countable            Uncountable

_____banana_____     _____rice_____

........................     ........................

........................     ........................

........................     ........................

**b** Look at these word pairs. Which word is countable and which is uncountable? Write C or U.

1  fruit      _U_          orange     _C_
2  sandwich   ...........   bread      ...........
3  beef       ...........   burger     ...........
4  coffee     ...........   café       ...........
5  shop       ...........   food       ...........
6  singer     ...........   music      ...........

**c** Complete the sentences with *a, an* or *some*.

1  I want to buy ___some___ shampoo at the chemist.

2  Let's go to the supermarket and get ............... food.

3  I'd like ............... orange, please.

4  I've got ............... sandwich and ............... fruit.

5  We need ............... rice and ............... onions.

6  It isn't ............... newsagent – it's ............... bookshop.

7  He wants ............... cheese and ............... apple.

**d** Write the words under the pictures with *a, an* or *some*.

1  ___a lettuce___      2  ...............

3  ...............      4  ...............

5  ...............      6  ...............

7  ...............      8  ...............

## ✱ this/that/these/those

**e** Complete the sentences with *this*, *that*, *these* or *those*.

1   There are some great CDs in ___that___ shop.

2   Mum! Look at _____ snails!

3   _____ apple's really good!

4   Wow! _____ players are really good!

5   _____ book's very expensive.

6   **Boy:**  What's _____ ?
    **Dad:**  It's a kangaroo.

## ✱ I'd like ... /Would you like ... ?

**f** <u>Underline</u> the correct words in the dialogue.

**Woman:**  Good morning. [1] <u>*Can I help you?*</u>  / *Would you like?*

**Man:**  Yes, [2] *I like / I'd like* three kilos of potatoes, please.

**Woman:**  Right. [3] *Do you like / Would you like* anything else?

**Man:**  Yes, [4] *I'd like / you'd like* some bananas – a kilo, please.

**Woman:**  Fine. That's £1.25, please. [5] *Do you like / Would you like* a bag?

**Man:**  Yes, please.

**9** Jane is in a restaurant. Put the waiter's words in order, and then write Jane's answers.

**Waiter:**  to / ready / you / Are / order

1   *Are you ready to order?* _____ ?

**Jane:** (yes / roast chicken)

2   _____

**Waiter:**  vegetables / like / or / you / salad / Would

3   _____ ?

**Jane:** (vegetables)

4   _____

**Waiter:**  drink / like / would / to / What / you

5   _____ ?

**Jane:** (orange juice)

6   _____

**Waiter:**  like / you / else / Would / anything

7   _____ ?

**Jane:** (no)

8   _____

## 4 Pronunciation

✴ /w/ would

**a** ► CD3 T21  Listen and repeat.

1  The Swiss waiter's got wavy hair.
2  We want some white wine.
3  William's got a wonderful dishwasher.
4  Would you like some water with your sandwich?

**b** ► CD3 T22  In these sentences, there are three words with a 'silent' *w*. <u>Underline</u> them, then listen, check and repeat.

1  Which answer is correct?
2  What's wrong with you?
3  Who's the winner?
4  Where does Wendy write letters?

## 5 Everyday English

Complete the dialogues. Use one word from Box A and Box B each time.

| A | |
|---|---|
| Yes | No |
| Oh | Don't |

| B | |
|---|---|
| right. | worry. |
| please. | thanks. |

## 6 Study help

✴ Grammar and vocabulary

**a** Put countable and uncountable nouns together in lists, for example:

a/an    *banana*                some    *cheese*
        *egg*                           *rice*

**b** Add these words to the two lists.

potato   water   meat   lettuce   mayonnaise   mushroom

**c** In your Vocabulary notebook, write all the words you know for food and drink in two lists: countable and uncountable nouns.

**d** A good dictionary gives symbols for countable and uncountable nouns. Look at these examples.

**garlic** /ˈgɑːlɪk/ *noun* [U] a vegetable like a small onion
**biscuit** /ˈbɪskɪt/ *noun* [C] a thin flat cake that is usually dry

1  A:  See the girl over there? She's from Italy.
   B:  ........................... That's interesting. Let's go and talk to her!

2  A:  This homework is really difficult! I can't do it.
   B:  ..........................., Steve. I can help you.

3  A:  Do you want an apple?
   B:  ........................... I'm hungry, and I love apples!

4  A:  Let's watch the football match on television.
   B:  Football? ........................... I don't like football at all!

# Skills in mind

## 7 Listen

**a** ▶CD3 T23 Listen to a conversation between Martin and his mother. What food have they got at home, and what haven't they got? Write ✔ or ✗.

1 chicken ✔

2 beef ☐

3 cheese ☐

4 lettuce ☐

5 tomatoes ☐

6 mayonnaise ☐

**b** What sandwich does Martin decide to have?

---

### WRITING TIP

*Writing lists*

Look at how you write lists of words.

*I like apples, oranges and grapes.*
*I want some eggs, some onions, a lettuce and some cheese.*

Notice the commas ( , ) and the use of *and* before the last thing in the list.

## 8 Write

**a** Martin and Harry are having a party at Harry's house on Saturday. Read Martin's email about food at the party.

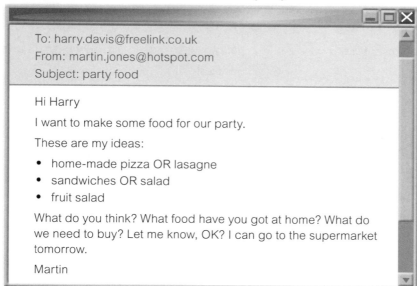

To: harry.davis@freelink.co.uk
From: martin.jones@hotspot.com
Subject: party food

Hi Harry

I want to make some food for our party.

These are my ideas:

• home-made pizza OR lasagne
• sandwiches OR salad
• fruit salad

What do you think? What food have you got at home? What do we need to buy? Let me know, OK? I can go to the supermarket tomorrow.

Martin

**b** Imagine you are Harry. Write an email in reply to Martin and answer his questions about food.

*Hi Martin*

*I like your ideas for party food. Let's have ...*

*At home I've got ...*

*I've also got ...*

*I want you to buy ...*

# Unit check

## 1 Fill in the spaces

Complete the sentences with the words in the box.

| vegetables | ~~beef~~ | dessert | sandwiches | meat | fruit | an | some | meal | have |

We always have roast ____*beef*____ or lamb for lunch on Sunday and it's my favourite ¹_____. We eat the ²_____ with potatoes and other ³_____, and then we have some ⁴_____ or ice cream for ⁵_____. On school days I don't ⁶_____ a big lunch. I make some ⁷_____ in the morning, and I eat them at lunchtime with ⁸_____ orange or ⁹_____ grapes. 

| 9 |

## 2 Choose the correct answers

(Circle) the correct answer: a, b or c.

1 A: I'm starving!
  B: _____
  a What's wrong?  b (Have a sandwich.)  c Do you think so?

2 Are you _____ to order?
  a ready  b hungry  c lovely

3 A: Have you got any vegetables?
  B: Yes, we've got some mushrooms and some _____.
  a oranges  b onions  c grapes

4 Does Tom want _____ apple?
  a a  b an  c some

5 I want a _____ for the salad.
  a salt  b mushroom  c lettuce

6 A: _____ you like some cheese?
  B: Yes, please.
  a Would  b Do  c Have

7 I'd like some _____, please.
  a rice  b strawberry  c chip

8 Do you know _____ woman in the white car?
  a this  b that  c these

9 These tomatoes are OK, but _____ bananas don't look fresh.
  a this  b that  c those 

| 8 |

## 3 Vocabulary

(Circle) the correct word in each sentence.

1 My sister is vegetarian, but she eats *beef* / (beans).
2 Don't put so much *salt / cereal* in your soup. That's not healthy.
3 In the morning, I always have *cereal / garlic* with some milk.
4 *Chocolate / Beans* is delicious, but don't eat too much of it.
5 I love *olive oil / yoghurt* with banana in it.
6 You can't eat raw *olive oil / beans*.
7 *Yoghurt / Garlic* has a strong smell, but it's very healthy.
8 I like salad with *cereal / olive oil* on top.
9 The spaghetti's very good – it just needs a little *salt / yoghurt* to make it delicious! 

| 8 |

## How did you do?

Total: | 25 |

 Very good 20 – 25     OK 13 – 19     Review Unit 6 again 0 – 12

# 7 I sometimes watch TV

## 1 Remember and check

Think back to the text about Calvin and Mawar. <u>Underline</u> the correct words.
Then check with the text on page 54 of the Student's Book.

1 Calvin and Mawar both live <u>far away from a big city</u> / in a city.
2 Calvin lives *on an island / in a village.*
3 He learns *in a school / at home.*
4 His mother *teaches Calvin / works in a factory.*

5 Mawar's home is in *Scotland / Java.*
6 She goes to school with *only a few children / 100 other children.*
7 She *likes / doesn't like* the school in her village.
8 Mawar's family *haven't got / have got* a TV.

## 2 Vocabulary

**✱ The days of the week**

**a** What are the words? Write the days of the week.

> ednwdsaye    yundas    iyfard    ustdeay    trusaayd    ~~ondmya~~    ytuhrsad

Weekdays: _Monday_ ................... ................... ................... ...................

Weekend: ................... ...................

**b** Match the days to the activities. Then answer the questions about Karen's week.

Mon        Tues        Wed        Thurs        Fri        Sat        Sun

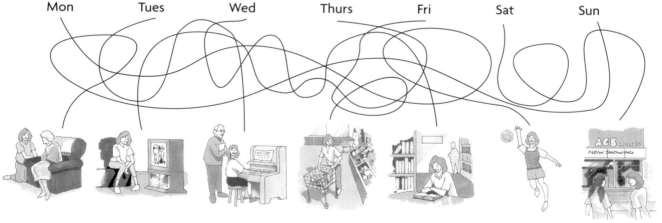

1 When does Karen go shopping?
  _On Friday._ ...................
2 When does Karen watch her favourite TV programme?
  ...................
3 When does she play volleyball?
  ...................
4 When does she see her grandmother?
  ...................
5 When does she have a music lesson?
  ...................

6 When does she study in the library?
  ...................
7 When does she go to the cinema?
  ...................

**c** Write four sentences about things you do on different days.

1 ...................
2 ...................
3 ...................
4 ...................

## 3 Grammar

★ Adverbs of frequency

**a** Put the adverbs in the correct order.

~~never~~   always   often   hardly ever   usually   sometimes

1 ............   2 ............   3 ............   4 ............   5 ............   6 _never_

**b** Put the adverbs in the correct place in the sentence.

1 Susan wears black shoes. (usually)

_Susan usually wears black shoes._

2 Robert plays football with his friends. (often)

...........................................................

3 Tony and Philip take the school bus. (never)

...........................................................

4 Beth listens to classical music. (hardly ever)

...........................................................

5 We have pizzas on Friday. (always)

...........................................................

6 The music is fantastic on this programme. (usually)

...........................................................

7 My parents help me with my homework. (sometimes)

...........................................................

**c** How often do you do these things? Write true sentences. Use adverbs from Exercise 3a.

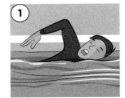    

go swimming on Sunday | have a burger at lunchtime | go to bed before ten o'clock | listen to the radio in bed | watch TV before school

1 _I often go swimming on Sunday._ ........................................

2 ...........................................................

3 ...........................................................

4 ...........................................................

5 ...........................................................

**d** Look at the information about Alex. Write sentences about him.

|  | Mon | Tues | Wed | Thur | Fri | Sat | Sun |
|---|---|---|---|---|---|---|---|
| have an English lesson |  | ✔ |  | ✔ |  | ✔ |  |
| play football |  |  |  |  |  | ✔ | ✔ |
| write letters |  |  |  |  |  |  | ✔ |
| walk to school | ✔ | ✔ | ✔ | ✔ | ✔ |  |  |

1 _Alex has an English lesson three times a week._

2 He ........................................................

...........................................................

3 ...........................................................

...........................................................

4 ...........................................................

...........................................................

**e** Write sentences with frequency expressions (for example, *twice a day, every morning*).

Matthew

Julie

Danny

Denise

Greg

1 *Matthew catches a train twice a day.*

2 ................................................

3 ................................................

4 ................................................

5 ................................................

## 4 Vocabulary

**✱** TV programmes

**a** (Circle) seven more kinds of TV programmes in the word snake.

newssoapoperachatshowcomedycartoongameshowdocumentarysportsprogramme

**b** Read about some programmes on TV tonight. Write the types of programmes.

1 Tonight, Mike Figgis talks to two great film stars.
   ......*chat show*......

2 We've got Italian football and skiing from Switzerland.
   ................................................

3 The latest information from around the world, with Sue Baxter. ................................................

4 Tonight – The Simpsons. ................................................

5 In tonight's programme, Mary sees Bill going out with Amanda – and she isn't happy about it!
   ................................................

6 Lots of laughs and smiles with the popular Benny Hall.
   ................................................

7 The prize tonight: £25,000!! ................................................

8 This week: Life in Japan. ................................................

## 5 Pronunciation

**✱** Compound nouns

**a** ▶CD3 T24 Add the words in the box to make new nouns. Listen and check.

| work | berry | paper | friend |
|------|-------|-------|--------|
| day | fly | ~~fast~~ | time |

1 break *fast* ............  5 straw............

2 week............  6 news............

3 lunch............  7 dragon............

4 home............  8 girl............

**b** ▶CD3 T24 Where is the stress in each word? Listen again and repeat.

# 6 Vocabulary

★ What's the time?

**a** Look at the pictures and write the times in list 1–6. Then match them with the other expressions in list a–g.

1 *It's seven thirty.*     a It's twenty-five to eight.

2 It's _____     b It's half past seven.

3 _____          c It's ten past seven.

4 _____          d It's quarter to eight.

5 _____          e It's ten to seven.

6 _____          f It's quarter past six.

**b** ▶CD3 T25  Listen and write the times in number form. Then listen again and check your answers.

1  *11.55*      2 _____   3 _____   4 _____   5 _____   6 _____

# 7 Culture in mind

Complete the summary about Claire Woods. Use the words in the box. Then check with the text on page 58 of the Student's Book.

> never   also   always   ~~lives~~   hardly ever   every day   sometimes

Claire is 16 and she [1] _____lives_____ in England. She doesn't watch television [2] _____ because she thinks it can be a waste of time. But she [3] _____ watches *Britain's Got Talent* – it's her favourite programme! She likes learning about other countries, so she [4] _____ watches documentaries.

At the weekend, she [5] _____ watches cartoons. She [6] _____ watches sports programmes – she doesn't like them at all. And she [7] _____ watches the news.

# 8 Study help

★ Grammar

**a** Look at the sentence. What part of speech is each word?

*Sam often wears white shoes.*

| Nouns | Verbs | Adjectives | Adverbs |
|-------|-------|------------|---------|
| shoes | wears | white | often |
| _____ | _____ | _____ | _____ |
| _____ | _____ | _____ | _____ |
| _____ | _____ | _____ | _____ |

**b** Look at the words in the box and add them to the lists.

> black   never   buys   sandwiches   sometimes
> coffee   always   delicious   has   expensive
> clothes   makes

**c** Make new sentences with the four parts of speech. There are lots of possible answers!

Sam *sometimes makes delicious sandwiches.*

Jill _____

Jack _____

Rosa _____

## 9 Read

**a** Read the text and choose the best title.

1 Television in a British family
2 Soap operas on British TV
3 Football programmes in Britain

TELEVISION is very important in a lot of British homes. On average, people spend about 23 hours a week in front of the TV. The nation's favourite programmes are soaps, but game shows, 'reality TV' shows, dramas and comedies are also popular. We talked to one family, the Parkers from Leeds, about how often they watch TV.

Simon Parker (42) isn't typical. He doesn't watch a lot of TV, but he usually watches the news and he sometimes watches a football match on Saturday. The two children love TV. Jamie (12) watches every day, usually for about three hours a day. His favourite programmes are cartoons and comedies. His sister Kim (16) watches three different soaps every week. 'I really love soaps, and chat shows are good too,' she says. Elizabeth Parker (38) likes watching TV at the weekend, when there's a good film on. 'I love old films,' she says. 'And I often watch documentaries too.'

Like a lot of British families, the Parkers have two televisions in their home, and the members of the family watch different things at different times. Do they watch anything together? 'Yes,' says Jamie. 'Football matches when England's playing!'

### READING TIP

*Choosing a title for a text*

In Exercise 9a, all the words in the three titles are in the text. But two of these aren't good titles because they go with only one small part of the text.

- Read the text from beginning to end before you decide about the title.
- Don't only look for words – think about general ideas.
- Remember, the title is for the *whole* text.

**b** Read the text again and answer the questions.

1 How much TV do British people watch?
   *About 23 hours per week.*

2 Does Mr Parker watch game shows?
   ............................................................

3 Which kinds of programmes does Jamie like?
   ............................................................

4 Does he watch TV seven days a week?
   ............................................................

5 What is Kim's favourite kind of programme?
   ............................................................

6 When does Mrs Parker watch films?
   ............................................................

7 What do the family watch together?
   ............................................................

## 10 Listen

**a** ▶CD3 T26 Listen to an interview about TV. How often does the woman watch television?
   ............................................................

**b** ▶CD3 T26 Listen again and tick (✔) the correct adverb.

|   | never | hardly ever | sometimes | usually |
|---|-------|-------------|-----------|---------|
| 1 comedies |  |  |  | ✔ |
| 2 documentaries |  |  |  |  |
| 3 soaps |  |  |  |  |
| 4 the news |  |  |  |  |

# Unit check

## 1 Fill in the spaces

Complete the sentences with the words in the box.

| on   at   every   usually   do   comes   news   ~~weekdays~~   days   soap |
|---|

On _weekdays_ I leave school [1]_____ 3.45 in the afternoon. I [2]_____ walk home with my friend Diane, but [3]_____ Wednesday I have a swimming lesson at the sports centre. Diane often [4]_____ round to my place and we watch our favourite [5]_____ – it's on at 5.30, five [6]_____ a week. We also watch the [7]_____ at 6 o'clock. I [8]_____ my homework after dinner [9]_____ evening, so I don't watch a lot of TV.

[ 9 ]

## 2 Choose the correct answers

(Circle) the correct answer: a, b or c.

1  We can get a lot of information from

    _____ .

    a (documentaries)   b comedies
    c soap operas

2  People try to win money on _____ .
    a chat shows   b game shows
    c sports programmes

3  Quarter past four is _____ .
    a 4.15   b 4.30   c 4.45

4  _____ the time?
    a When's   b What's   c Where's

5  10.40 is _____ .
    a forty past ten   b twenty to eleven
    c twenty past eleven

6  The day before Thursday is _____ .
    a Wednesday   b Friday   c Monday

7  Sandra isn't at home. She _____ goes shopping on Saturday.
    a never   b hardly ever   c always

8  I check my email three times _____ day.
    a the   b a   c of the

9  _____ do you watch soap operas?
    a Which   b How many   c How often

[ 8 ]

## 3 Vocabulary

Choose a word or phrase from the box to complete each sentence. There are three words or phrases you don't need.

| ten past ten   twenty-five to ten   Wednesday ~~chat shows~~   Monday   news   game show comedy   Saturday   cartoons   documentaries sports programme |
|---|

1  My sister loves _chat shows_ . She thinks it's great when big stars talk about their lives.

2  My mum is in a _____ next week. I hope she wins a lot of money!

3  I always watch the _____ . I want to know what's going on in the world.

4  I love _____ . It's interesting to learn how people in other countries live.

5  It's ten to nine now. In forty-five minutes it's

    _____ .

6  My favourite day is _____ . I can stay up and watch the late night film because on Sunday I can sleep longer.

7  I love the weekend, and I always find it difficult to get up on _____ morning.

8  My favourite programme is called *Just for laughs* – it's a _____ , and it's very funny.

9  I don't like _____ very much. I think they are for young children.

[ 8 ]

## How did you do?

Total: [ 25 ]

| 😊 | Very good 20 – 25 | 😐 | OK 13 – 19 | 🙁 | Review Unit 7 again 0 – 12 |
|---|---|---|---|---|---|

# 8 Don't do that!

## 1 Remember and check

▶ **CD3 T27** Can you complete the dialogue between Julie and Steve? Complete the sentences. Then listen and check.

**Steve:** This film's [1] ____*awful*____ . I'm bored. Really bored.

**Julie:** Me too. And I'm [2] _____ – I mean, I don't understand the story. What's that?

**Steve:** What?

**Julie:** That noise. What is it?

**Steve:** Hmm. I don't know. Stay [3] _____ .

**Julie:** Don't go outside! I'm [4] _____ .

**Steve:** Don't [5] _____ , Julie. Everything's OK.

**Julie:** Steve? Where are you? Come [6] _____ !

**Julie:** Help!

**Steve:** It's me!

**Julie:** Oh Steve – you [7] _____ ! Don't do that!

**Steve:** Sorry, Julie. It's just a joke.

**Julie:** Oh Steve. Sometimes you're really, really [8] _____ .

## 2 Grammar

### ✱ Negative imperatives

**a** Complete the dialogues with the verbs in the box.

> be   laugh   shout   cry

1 **A:** What's the matter, Cynthia?
   **B:** It's awful here. I miss my friends at home.
   **A:** I know you're unhappy. But please don't _____ .

2 **A:** That's the new boy, Klaus. He's from Germany.
   **B:** His English is really funny!
   **A:** Don't _____ at his English. You don't speak German!

3 **A:** Hi, Mum! I'm home!
   **B:** Shhh! Don't _____ ! Your dad's asleep!

4 **A:** I want to take a photo of you in front of the museum.
   **B:** Oh no! I hate photos of myself!
   **A:** Don't _____ stupid! Come on!

**b** Read the text. Complete the advice with the verbs in the box.

> Ask   ~~Listen~~   Don't eat   Go   Listen
> Write   Don't tell   Talk   Don't sit

## Advice for teens

**When you or your friends are in trouble …**

**We all have good and bad days. When you have a problem, here are some things you can do:**

- ____*Listen*____ to music and try to relax.

- [1] _____ the problem on a piece of paper. Then make a list of things you can do and put them in order.

- [2] _____ a lot of food – it doesn't make you feel better.

- [3] _____ in the house.
  [4] _____ for a walk – exercise is good for you.

- [5] _____ to a friend about your problem.

**What can you do when a friend has a problem? Here are some ideas:**

- [6] _____ to your friend – don't speak a lot.

- [7] _____ questions. Help your friend to talk openly.

- Your friend's problem is private.
  [8] _____ other people about it.

**C** Look at the pictures and write sentences. Use the positive or negative form of the verbs in the box.

look at ~~eat~~ go open switch on talk

①  ②  ③

④  ⑤  ⑥

1  *Eat your vegetables.*

2  *Don't* ................................................................................

3  ................................................................................

4  ................................................................................

5  ................................................................................

6  ................................................................................

## ③ Pronunciation

### ✳ Linking sounds

**▶CD3 T28** In these sentences, <u>underline</u> the word *don't* when you think the *t* is silent. Then listen, check and repeat.

1  I <u>don't</u> know why she isn't here.

2  Don't leave me now.

3  Don't play the music. I don't like it.

4  Please don't ask a lot of questions.

5  I don't understand why he's so angry.

6  Don't eat all the chocolate!

7  Don't open the box.

8  I don't think it's a good idea.

# ④ Vocabulary

✱ How do you feel?

**a** In the puzzle, find seven more words to describe feelings. Write the words under the pictures (1–8).

| A | E | X | C | I | T | E | D | W | W |
|---|---|---|---|---|---|---|---|---|---|
| A | R | W | O | R | R | I | E | D | O |
| S | R | U | N | S | A | D | P | J | R |
| C | F | F | F | H | H | A | I | S | B |
| A | G | I | U | A | F | N | P | A | O |
| R | N | Z | S | P | J | G | L | H | R |
| E | E | T | E | P | N | R | Q | A | E |
| D | X | C | D | Y | G | Y | W | P | D |

1 ...........................

2 ...........................

3 ...........................

4 ........... *excited* .........

**b** Underline the correct words.

1 Look! There's a snake! I'm *angry / scared*.

2 This lesson's awful. We're *bored / scared*.

3 Our teacher smiles a lot. She's always *happy / sad*.

4 I don't know what to do. I'm *happy / confused*.

5 It's my little sister's birthday tomorrow. She's really *excited / angry*.

6 My father's got a problem. He's *worried / happy*.

7 Lee hasn't got any friends here. He's *excited / sad*.

8 I haven't got my homework with me. The teacher's *angry / confused*.

5 ...........................

6 ...........................

7 ...........................

8 ...........................

**c** ▶CD3 T29 Listen to the five speakers. Match them with the feelings and the reasons why they feel this way. Then write sentences.

| Speaker | Feeling | Why? |
|---|---|---|
| 1 George | confused | There's a problem with the computer. |
| 2 Hazel | worried | She's the winner of a trip to the USA. |
| 3 Carl | bored | It's late and her daughter isn't home. |
| 4 Fiona | angry | He hasn't got anything to do. |
| 5 Mark | excited | The homework is difficult. |

1 *George is bored because he hasn't got anything to do.*

2 *Hazel* ...........................................................

3 ...........................................................

4 ...........................................................

5 ...........................................................

**d** Look at these examples.

*We're inter<u>ested</u> in these books.* (describes a person's feeling)

*These books are interest<u>ing</u>.* (describes something that produces a feeling)

**Complete the dialogues with adjectives from the box.**

> confused confusing excited exciting
> worried worrying bored boring

1 A: This film's _____ .
  B: I think so too. Let's switch off the TV.

2 A: My grandmother is in hospital.
  B: Oh no! Really?
  A: Yes, we're all very
     _____ about her.

3 A: What's the answer to question 3? I don't understand it.
  B: I have no idea. I think the question's very _____ .

4 A: Why is the dog so
     _____ ?
  B: Because she knows Leo's coming. He always takes her for a walk in the afternoon.

**e** **Vocabulary bank** What are the words? Complete the sentences.

1 There's an important test this morning, so I'm feeling very <u>srsstdee</u> ___<u>stressed</u>___ .

2 I can't find my cat! I'm very <u>stpeu</u> _____ about it.

3 Don't be <u>itedfngher</u> _____ ! This dog is very friendly!

4 I'm not worried about the test! I'm very <u>deerlax</u> _____ about it!

5 It's very late and I'm feeling <u>eplyse</u> _____ . I think it's time to go to bed!

6 This film isn't funny. I'm not <u>medusa</u> _____ at all.

## 5 Everyday English

<u>Underline</u> the correct words.

1 A: Do you like spaghetti bolognese?
  B: Yes, *the thing is / I think* it's delicious.

2 A: *What's wrong / The thing is*, Alex?
  B: I'm very tired. Really tired!

3 A: Let's listen to this CD.
  B: No thanks. It's late, and *anyway / I think*, I don't really like that CD.

4 A: Let's go to the cinema tonight.
  B: No, thanks.
  A: Why not?
  B: Well, *I think / the thing is*, I haven't got any money.

## 6 Study help

**✶ Vocabulary**

In your Vocabulary notebook write examples to help you learn how to use new words. For example:

excited  (I feel <u>excited</u> before a big party.)
bored   (I feel <u>bored</u> when I watch golf on TV.)

**Think of your own example sentences for these adjectives.**

excited (_____
_____ )

scared  (_____
_____ )

bored   (_____
_____ )

worried (_____
_____ )

happy   (_____
_____ )

## 7 Read

Read Jennifer's letter to a magazine and write *T* (true) or *F* (false).

### Claire's PROBLEM PAGE

Dear Claire,

I'm fourteen and I'm really unhappy. Please help me!

My mum, my brother and I have moved from London to San Diego in California. My mum is a computer programmer and she's got a new job at the university here. We live in a new house, and I go to a new school. It's a nice place – but everything is new for me! New teachers, new students in my class, new school work! I really miss my old friends from London. I even miss my teachers there! And I'm worried about my school work – sometimes I'm confused because it's different from the work at my old school.

I feel very alone – but what can I do? Please don't tell me to talk to my mum. She works eight hours a day and she's always tired. She never has time for me. And my brother? He's only ten, so he can't help me.

San Diego is a nice city, but there are so many things I miss! Please tell me what to do.

Yours,

Jennifer

## 8 Write

Imagine you are Claire. Write an answer to Jennifer – tell her what to do!

*Dear Jennifer*

*I'm sorry you're sad and I understand your problem. Here are some ideas. ......*

### WRITING TIP

*Planning your writing*

Before you write to Jennifer, make notes about the things you want to say to her. Organise your ideas under these headings:

| General ideas | Friends | School work |
|---|---|---|
| | Keeping old friends | |
| | Making new friends | |

1  Jennifer isn't happy and she needs some help.  [ T ]

2  She and her family live in London.  [  ]

3  Her mother works in a computer shop.  [  ]

4  Jennifer doesn't miss her old friends.  [  ]

5  She has problems with her studies at school.  [  ]

6  Jennifer's mother doesn't talk to her about her problems.  [  ]

7  Jennifer often talks to her brother.  [  ]

# Unit check

## 1 Fill in the spaces

Complete the dialogue with the words in the box.

| matter | listen | ~~you~~ | help | angry | happy | worried | don't | fine | boyfriend |

Rosa: Are ___you___ OK, Lynn? You don't look very [1]_____ .

Lynn: Oh, I'm [2]_____ .

Rosa: Come on. What's the [3]_____ ?

Lynn: Oh, I'm [4]_____ with Janet Martin. She's saying bad things about my [5]_____ .

Rosa: Lynn, don't [6]_____ to her. She's stupid.

Lynn: Yes, I guess you're right.

Rosa: Look, [7]_____ think about her. Come round to my place and [8]_____ me
with my English. I'm [9]_____ about the test tomorrow.

Lynn: OK, let's go.

| 9 |

## 2 Choose the correct answers

Circle the correct answer: a, b or c.

1 I think this music is _____ .
a **boring** b bored c worried

2 Is this word right or wrong? I'm _____ .
a confused b excited c scared

3 Tom's _____ because his pet budgie is dead.
a angry b worried c sad

4 Switch _____ the television, please.
a in b on c up

5 Laura's a happy person. She smiles and _____ a lot.
a shouts b cries c laughs

6 Go _____ ! I'm trying to listen to the radio.
a over b away c straight on

7 Please don't go! _____ here!
a Is b Back c Stay

8 Please leave me _____ .
a alone b around c about

9 I don't want to talk to you. _____ me again.
a Call b Phone c Don't phone

| 8 |

## 3 Vocabulary

In each sentence, underline the word that does not fit.

1 My friend Alex smiles a lot. He's very *happy / relaxed / unhappy*.

2 This is a very bad film. I'm really *bored / excited / confused*.

3 Mum's got a problem. She's *worried / unhappy / happy*.

4 We talk in lessons. The teacher gets *angry / scared / unhappy*.

5 I hate really big dogs. I'm *frightened / scared / bored* of them.

6 It's my birthday tomorrow. I'm *excited / happy / sleepy*.

7 My sister's rabbit is dead. She's very *excited / upset / unhappy*.

8 This test is easy! I'm really *angry / relaxed / happy*!

9 My uncle is in hospital. He's very ill. I'm very *upset / worried / bored*.

| 8 |

## How did you do?

Total: | | 25

 Very good 20 – 25  OK 14 – 19  Review Unit 8 again 0 – 13

# 9 Yes, I can

## 1 Remember and check

Complete the summary of the text about Rick Hoyt.
Use the verbs in the box. Then check with the text on
page 68 of the Student's Book.

> swim   uses   ride   pulls   take part   ~~works~~   sits   pushes

Rick Hoyt has got cerebral palsy, but he <sup>1</sup> ___*works*___
in a university and he <sup>2</sup> _____ a computer to
communicate. Rick and his father also <sup>3</sup> _____
in triathlons together. Rick can't run, so his father
<sup>4</sup> _____ him in a wheelchair. He can't
<sup>5</sup> _____ , so his father <sup>6</sup> _____ him
through the water in a boat. And he can't <sup>7</sup> _____
a bike, so he <sup>8</sup> _____ in a seat on the front of his
father's bike.

## 2 Grammar

✱ *can / can't* (ability)

**a** Look at the pictures. Write a sentence for each picture.

1  _She can sing._

2  _____

3  _____

4  _____

5  _____

6  _____

**b** Write questions for the activities in Exercise 2a.
Start with *Can you ...?* Then write true answers
(*Yes, I can / No, I can't*).

1  _Can you sing?_
_____

2  _____

3  _____
_____

4  _____

5  _____

6  _____

**c** Look at the information in the table and complete the sentences.

| | | | | |
|---|---|---|---|---|
| Sylvia | ✔ | ✘ | ✘ | ✘ |
| Paul | ✔ | ✔ | ✘ | ✔ |
| George | ✔ | ✘ | ✔ | ✔ |
| Eva | ✘ | ✔ | ✘ | ✘ |

1 A: _____*Can*_____ George walk on his hands?

   B: _*No*_ , he _____*can't*_____ .

2 Sylvia _____ stand on her head, but she _____ walk on her hands.

3 Paul and George _____ juggle.

4 Sylvia, Paul and Eva _____ ride a horse.

5 A: _____ Sylvia and Eva juggle?

   B: _____ , they _____ .

6 A: _____ Paul and Sylvia walk on their hands?

   B: Paul _____ , but Sylvia _____ .

**d** Make true sentences. Use your own ideas.

1 I can't _____ , but
  I can _____ .

2 I can _____ , but
  I can't _____ .

3 My parents can _____
  _____ , but they can't _____
  _____ .

4 My best friend can _____
  _____ , but he/she can't _____
  _____ .

5 A chimpanzee can't _____
  _____ , but it can _____
  _____ .

6 Young children can _____
  _____ , but they can't _____
  _____ .

## ❸ Pronunciation

✶ *can / can't*

**a** ▶CD3 T30 Listen to the questions and answers. Underline the words that are stressed.

1 Can you <u>read</u>?      <u>Yes</u>, I <u>can</u>.

2 Can they write?      Yes, they can.

3 Can she play the guitar?      Yes, she can.

**b** ▶CD3 T30 Listen again. This time, listen to the pronunciation of *can*. Is it the same in the questions and the answers?

**c** ▶CD3 T31 Read these sentences. Underline the words that you think are stressed. Then listen, check and repeat.

1 I can dance, but I can't sing.

2 He can read, but he can't write.

3 Can she play the piano?

4 Can you do Sudoku puzzles?

## 4 Vocabulary

**✱ Sports**

**a** Look at the pictures and complete the sentences.

1 John _plays volleyball_ with his friends.
2 People _____ here in the winter.
3 We _____ once a week.
4 Can James _____ ?
5 Kate _____ in the park.
6 People sometimes _____ in this river.
7 Can you _____ ?
8 We often _____ after school.

**b** Look at these lists. Complete them with more sports.

| go + -ing | play + name of game | do |
|-----------|---------------------|-----|
| go skiing | play tennis | do sport |
| go riding | | |
| | | |
| | | |

**c** [Vocabulary bank] Underline the correct word.

1 He's a *fan* / *referee*.

2 The *score* / *team* is two-nil.

3 It's a *draw* / *third*.

| Arsenal | 2 |
|---------|---|
| Stoke | 0 |

4 My team is Stoke. They always *win* / *lose*!

| New York | 95 |
|----------|----|
| Orlando | 102 |

5 My team is Orlando. They always *win* / *lose*!

6 They're very happy – they're the *fans* / *champions*!

## 5 Grammar

**✱ like / don't like -ing**

**a** Look at the information about the people. Write sentences about them using these verbs:

| | Joanna | Kevin | Brian and Louise |
|---|---|---|---|
| 😁 = love | 🙂 (skiing) | ☹️ (riding) | ☹️ (boxing) |
| 🙂 = like | 😁 (swimming) | ☹️ (gymnastics) | ☹️ (guitar) |
| 😐 = not like | 😐 (football) | 😁 (running) | 😁 (computer) |
| 😠 = hate | 😠 (football) | 🙂 (handball) | 🙂 (reading) |

1 *Joanna likes skiing. She loves swimming, but she doesn't like rollerblading. She hates playing football.*

2 Kevin _____

3 Brian and Louise _____

56 UNIT 9

**b** Write similar sentences about you, your best friend and people in your family.

1 I ..............................................................

2 My best friend ..............................................................

3 My ..............................................................

4 My ..............................................................

## 6 Culture in mind

**a** Match the names of the sports with the pictures. Write the numbers 1–6 in the boxes.

1 ~~rowing~~  2 hockey
3 netball  4 football
5 orienteering  6 cricket

A

B

C

D MAP

E

F 1

**b** Who does which sports? Write the sports from Exercise 6a under the names. Then check with the text on page 72 of the Student's Book.

Julia                    Paul

..................           ..................

..................           ..................

..................           ..................

## 7 Study help

★ Pronunciation

**a** For help with pronunciation, group words under their sounds. For example:

| /æ/ | /ɑː/ | /eɪ/ |
|-----|------|------|
| sad | park | race |
| match | basketball | holiday |
| .......... | .......... | .......... |
| .......... | .......... | .......... |
| .......... | .......... | .......... |

Add these words from Units 9 and 10 to the lists.

part  camel  rollerblade  strange  grass  gymnastics
laugh  fantastic  late

**b** Look for words in Units 8 and 9 to write under these sounds. If you aren't sure of the pronunciation, check in your dictionary.

| /ɪ/ | /iː/ | /ɒ/ | /əʊ/ |
|-----|------|-----|------|
| swim | team | hop | open |
| finish | wheelchair | problem | photo |
| ......... | ......... | ......... | ......... |
| ......... | ......... | ......... | ......... |
| ......... | ......... | ......... | ......... |

## 8 Listen

▶ **CD3 T32** Listen and choose the correct picture. Circle the correct answer A, B or C.

1 What sports does Tom do?

    A          B         Ⓒ

2 What can Cristina do?

    A          B         C

3 What does Matt do in the winter?

    A          B         C

4 What can't Pete do?

    A          B         C

## 9 Listen and write

**a** ▶ **CD3 T33** Listen to an interview with Mark Cavalcanti. Complete the information in the box.

**b** Use the information in the box to write a paragraph about Mark.

Name: _____*Mark Cavalcanti*_____

Age: [1] _____

Language(s): [2] _____

Nationality: [3] _____

His main sport: [4] _____

His other sports:

[5] _____

[6] _____

People in his family:

*Helen (mother)* _____

*Anna* [7] ( _____ )

Their sporting interests:

Helen: [8] _____

Anna: [9] _____

# Unit check

## 1 Fill in the spaces

Complete the sentences with the words in the box.

| team   can   swim   doesn't   loves   races   ~~sport~~   free   guitar   hockey |

Jackie is very good at _____ sport _____ . She can play [1]_____ and she's in the basketball [2]_____ at school. She can also [3]_____ well and she often wins [4]_____ on sports days. Her brother Tim does different things in his [5]_____ time. He [6]_____ juggle and walk on his hands and he [7]_____ playing the [8]_____ , but he [9]_____ like doing sport.

☐ 9

## 2 Choose the correct answers

Circle the correct answer: a, b or c.

1  I _____ mushrooms. I think they're awful.

   a like   b love   c (hate)

2  _____ is my favourite sport.

   a Rugby   b Singing   c Juggling

3  We often go _____ in winter.

   a netball   b skiing   c football

4  John _____ gymnastics twice a week after school.

   a goes   b plays   c does

5  They want to take part _____ the triathlon.

   a with   b for   c in

6  I _____ swim, but not very well.

   a can   b can't   c like

7  Barbara doesn't like team games, but she likes _____ .

   a rollerblading   b hockey   c volleyball

8  Can you _____ a bike?

   a ride   b run   c go

9  It _____ 20 minutes to walk to school.

   a has   b takes   c does

☐ 8

## 3 Vocabulary

Complete each sentence with a word from the box. There are two words you don't need.

| come   cycling   do   draw   go   play   ride   score   rugby   swimming   ~~volleyball~~ |

1  Let's go to the beach and play _____ volleyball _____ .

2  In the winter, we _____ skiing in the mountains. It's great!

3  In the summer, we go _____ in the river near our house.

4  It's a nice day – I want to _____ tennis with Julie.

5  It's a very exciting game – the _____ is 5–3!

6  At my school, we all _____ sport twice a week.

7  It's 2–2 – it's a _____ .

8  I'm a very good runner – I always _____ first in races at school.

9  I really love _____ – but my bike isn't very good.

☐ 8

## How did you do?

Total: ☐ 25

| :) Very good 20 – 25 | :| OK 14 – 19 | :( Review Unit 9 again 0 – 13 |

# 10 A bad storm's coming

## 1 Remember and check

Choose the correct words. Then check with the text on page 74 of the Student's Book.

1 John White is a *taxi* / *bus* driver.
2 John goes sailing *once* / *twice* a year with his wife and son.
3 This year John is sailing round *Britain* / *the world*.

4 Pauline phones John. He is near *South Africa* / *South America*.
5 John can see *whales* / *dolphins* outside his boat.
6 John stops talking because *a storm is coming* / *he's having breakfast*.

## 2 Grammar

✱ Present continuous

**a** Write the verbs in the *-ing* form and put them in the lists. Think about the spelling.

> come sit watch play
> swim write shop do
> use eat have run

**+ ing**

_____ *watching* _____
_____
_____
_____

**e + ing**

_____ *coming* _____
_____
_____
_____

**double letter + ing**

_____ *sitting* _____
_____
_____
_____

**b** Complete the answers. Use the present continuous form of the verbs from Exercise 2a.

1 **Max:** Where's James?
  **Peggy:** He's in his room. ___*He's playing*___ computer games.

2 **Norma:** Is Barbara at home?
  **Cynthia:** No, sorry. She's in town. _____ at the supermarket.

3 **Chris:** Where are Mum and Dad?
  **Peter:** They're in the living room. _____ a video.

4 **Caroline:** Do you want to go for a walk?
  **Richard:** No, not right now. _____ some postcards.

5 **Monica:** I can't see Nick and Petra.
  **Phil:** They're over there. _____ on that seat under the tree.

6 **Dad:** Tony and Frank, where are you?
  **Tony:** We're up here. _____ our homework.

7 **Dad:** Is Mum at home?
  **Kate:** Yes, she's in the bathroom. _____ a shower.

**c** Look at the picture. Correct these false statements.

1  Anne and Peter are playing cards.  *Peter isn't playing cards. He's reading.*

2  George and Alice are eating fish.

3  Dorothy is talking to George.

4  Maria and Bill are listening to music.

5  Pat is dancing.

6  Martin, Wendy and Lisa are playing the guitar.

**d** Make present continuous questions. Then write the short answers.

1  Mum and Dad / sit in the garden?

   *Are Mum and Dad sitting in the garden?*

   ✔ *Yes, they are.*

2  you / watch the news?

   ✗

3  Helen / do her homework?

   ✔

4  Ken and Neil / play tennis?

   ✗

5  Joe / use the computer?

   ✗

**e** Write true answers. Use the present continuous.

1  Where are you sitting at the moment?

2  What are you doing?

3  What are you using?

4  Are you sitting alone in the room?

5  Are you wearing glasses?

6  What are other people doing?

✻ Present continuous and present simple

**f** Look at these examples. Then underline the correct words in the sentences.

*Janet often **goes** to the market on Saturday, but this morning she's **playing** basketball.*

*I'm **having** pizza for lunch today, but I usually **have** sandwiches.*

1 My sister *talks / is talking* to Sophie on the phone. *They sometimes talk / They're sometimes talking* for over an hour!

2 *I read / I'm reading* a lot. At the moment *I read / I'm reading* a book about Russia.

3 A: Are Philip and Greg at home?
   B: No, *they play / they're playing* tennis. *They play / They're playing* three times a week.

4 A: Where's Eva?
   B: *She visits / She's visiting* her aunt and uncle. *She often stays / She's often staying* with them at the weekend.

5 A: How does your brother get to work?
   B: *He catches / He's catching* a train. But he *doesn't work / isn't working* this week – he's on holiday.

# ③ Pronunciation

✻ /h/ *have*

▶**CD3 T34** Listen and repeat.

1 Harry's hobby is horse-riding.
2 I'm hardly ever hungry at home.
3 He's unhappy about his hair.
4 How often does Helen help you?
5 Hannah's having a hamburger at the Hilton Hotel.

# ④ Vocabulary

✻ House and furniture

**a** Fill in the crossword.

Across
1 ... 3 ... 6 ...
7 ... 8 ... 9 ...

Down
1 ... 2 ... 4 ...
5 ... 7 ...

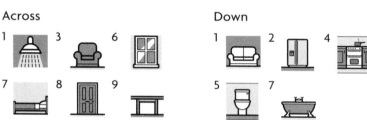

**b** Write the names of the rooms.

1 My family watches TV in this room. _living room_
2 We wash and have a shower in this room. _____
3 I sleep in this room. _____
4 There's a cooker and a fridge in this room. _____
5 The front door opens into this small room. _____

**c** **Vocabulary bank** Match the words and pictures.

1 a drawer
2 a hanger
3 a shelf
4 a lamp
5 curtains
6 a mirror
7 a blanket
8 a pillow

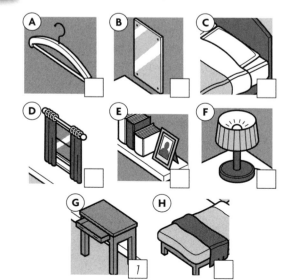

**✱ Prepositions**

**d** ▶CD3 T35 Listen and complete the text with the prepositions. Then draw the missing things in the picture of the room (table, window, computer, pictures, door).

on ~~in~~ near between next to under

I've got a bed and a desk _in_ my room. There's a small table ¹_____ the bed. The desk is ²_____ the window and I've got my computer ³_____ the desk. There's a small armchair in the corner of the room. On the wall ⁴_____ the desk and the armchair I've got three pictures of my favourite pop stars. The door is ⁵_____ the armchair.

## 5 Everyday English

Complete the dialogues. Use one word from Box A and Box B each time.

A Why don't all a bit lots     B of you right of

1 A: I don't like the teachers here. What do you think?

   B: Actually, I think there are _____ great teachers at this school.

2 A: Please, please help me with this homework! Please!

   B: Oh, _____ . Give me the book. What's the problem?

3 A: Oh, I'm really, really hungry!

   B: Are you? _____ eat an apple or a banana?

4 A: Would you like some soup, and then some chicken?

   B: No soup, thanks — but I'd like _____ chicken, please.

## 6 Study help

**✱ Vocabulary**

A good way to remember words is to draw a spidergram. Complete this spidergram.

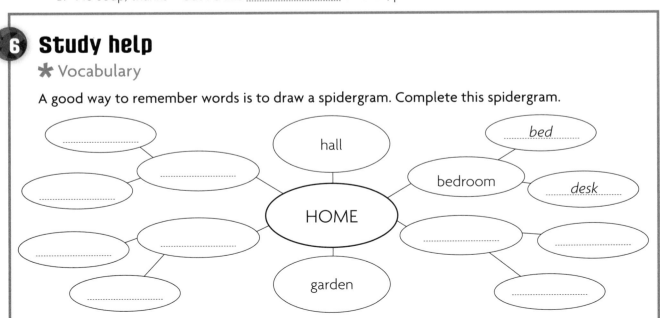

## 7 Read and listen

**a** Sue is on a school trip in Italy. Read her postcard to her parents. In the table, write ✔ (good) or ✗ (not good) under 'Sue'.

Empoli ▪ Florence

12th April

Dear Mum and Dad,

I'm writing this in Florence.
The city's lovely, but it's raining at
the moment. We're staying in a hotel,
but the rooms aren't very nice –
they're too small and dark. I'm not
doing very well with my Italian, but
I'm trying! The food's delicious and
we're all having a good time.

Lots of love,

Sue

33.PZA    02.12
ITALIA

Mr and Mrs Castle
32 Bridge Road
CAMBRIDGE
CB1 3FJ
Inghilterra

|   |                      | Sue (Florence) | Emma (Empoli) |
|---|----------------------|----------------|---------------|
| 1 | Hotel                | ✗              | ✔             |
| 2 | Speaking the language |                |               |
| 3 | Food                 |                |               |
| 4 | Weather              |                |               |
| 5 | Having a good time?  |                |               |

**b** ▶CD3 T36 Emma is also on the school trip. It's three days later and they're in Empoli. Listen to Emma talking to her father. In the table, write ✔ (good) or ✗ (not good) under 'Emma'.

## 8 Write

Imagine you're a tourist on holiday in your town. Write a postcard to your parents or to a friend. Use the topics from the table on this page.

### WRITING TIP

*Writing a postcard*

- Start with *Dear* _____ ,
- Here are some endings you can use.

  All the best,
  Love,
  Lots of love,
  Love from …

# Unit check

## 1 Fill in the spaces

Complete the sentences with the words in the box.

| in | is | aren't | are | finishing | reading | ~~sitting~~ | they're | living | bedroom |

At the moment, Jill's _____sitting_____ in front of the computer in her [1]_____ . She's [2]_____
her homework and her cat Sammy [3]_____ sleeping on her bed. Her two brothers [4]_____
watching a cricket match in the [5]_____ room and her sister is [6]_____ a book [7]_____
the garden. Their parents [8]_____ here because [9]_____ visiting some friends this afternoon.

**9**

## 2 Choose the correct answers

(Circle) the correct answer: a, b or c.

1 Dad's in the _____ . He's having a shower.
   a (bathroom)   b kitchen   c dining room

2 There's a new _____ in the kitchen.
   a bed   b sofa   c cooker

3 Put the milk in the _____ , please.
   a fridge   b bath   c toilet

4 Helen is in Poland. She's _____ a great time.
   a doing   b having   c making

5 Don't switch off the TV. Jack and I _____
   watching this film.
   a am   b is   c are

6 Listen! Susan _____ the violin.
   a play   b plays   c 's playing

7 _____ the computer at the moment?
   a Are you use   b You're using   c Are you using

8 What _____ today?
   a 's the weather like   b 's the weather liking
   c does the weather like

9 John and Alex are talking, but Pauline _____
   listening.
   a aren't   b isn't   c not

**8**

## 3 Vocabulary

Underline the word that is different from the others.

1 armchair   sofa   <u>bed</u>
2 garden   bedroom   kitchen
3 fridge   shower   bath
4 garage   cooker   fridge
5 window   kitchen   living room
6 table   chair   hall
7 garage   door   window
8 shelf   pillow   blanket
9 floor   hanger   ceiling

**8**

## How did you do?

Total: **25**

| | Very good 20 – 25 | | OK 14 – 19 | | Review Unit 10 again 0 – 13 |

# 11 Special days

## 1 Remember and check

Complete the sentences with the words in the box.
Then check on page 82 of the Student's Book.

> blouses   bread   celebrate   dancing   dinner   holiday
> ~~poet~~   skirt

- Every year on 25 January, the Scots remember a famous
  [1] _poet_ called Robert Burns. There is usually a special
  [2] _____ , and people eat haggis.

- Hogmanay is an important [3] _____ for the Scottish people.
  It is on the 31 December, and people [4] _____ with a party.
  They visit the homes of their friends and take a piece of
  [5] _____ and a piece of coal.

- At the Highland Games, men wear kilts (a kind of [6] _____ )
  and women wear skirts, [7] _____ and scarves. The bands play
  music and there is [8] _____ .

## 2 Vocabulary

✳ Months of the year and seasons

**a** Fill in the puzzle with months of the year (1–9).
What's the other month (10)?

..............................................

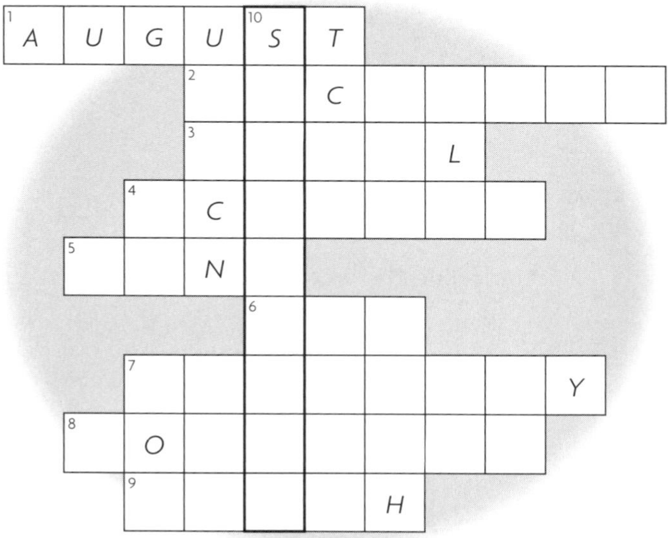

**b** Which two months aren't in the puzzle?

..............................   ..............................

**c** Answer the questions.

1   What month is your birthday?

..............................................

2   What month is your mother's birthday?

..............................................

3   Name a month when you don't go to school.

..............................................

4   Which months are cold in your country?

..............................................

5   Which is your favourite month? Why?

..............................................

**d** Write the names of the seasons (J = January, etc.).

1   J + F + M   =   ..............................................
2   A + M + J   =   ..............................................
3   J + A + S   =   ..............................................
4   O + N + D   =   ..............................................

Puzzle (across entries):
1   A U G U S T
2   · · C · · · ·
3   · · · L
4   · C · · ·
5   · N
6
7   · · · · Y
8   O · · ·
9   · · H

**e** What do you do in the four seasons?
Write a sentence for each season.

*In winter I play hockey and I sometimes
go skiing.*

..............................................
..............................................
..............................................
..............................................

## 3 Grammar

**✱ Prepositions**

**Complete the paragraph with *in*, *on* or *at*.**

In my country, the school year begins ¹__in__ February. My school day starts ²_____ 8.40, so I get up ³_____ 7 o'clock. That's fine when the weather's nice, but it isn't so good ⁴_____ winter. There are usually seven lessons a day, but ⁵_____ Wednesday we always have sport in the afternoon. School finishes at 3.45, but ⁶_____ Thursday I stay until 5 o'clock to play netball with the junior team. We have our long holiday ⁷_____ summer – it begins ⁸_____ December and I usually go away with my family for two weeks ⁹_____ January.

## 4 Vocabulary

**✱ Clothes**

**a** What are the words? Write the clothes in the pictures.

| osehs | serds | tkejac | risht | anjes | peumjr | riantser | ~~opt~~ | srutores | cossk | frasc | hitTrs |
|---|---|---|---|---|---|---|---|---|---|---|---|

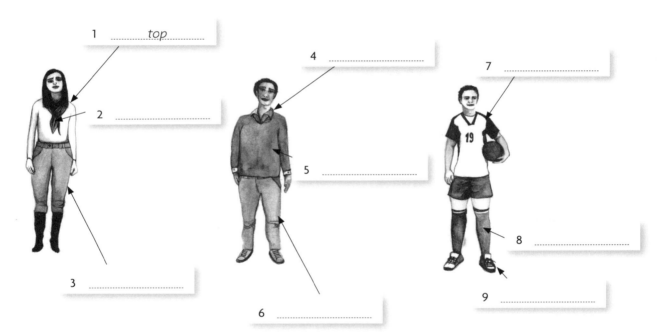

1 _____top_____

2 _____

3 _____

4 _____

5 _____

6 _____

7 _____

8 _____

9 _____

**b** Write true answers to these questions.

1 What do you usually wear to school?

..................................................................

2 What are your favourite clothes?

..................................................................

3 What clothes do you hate wearing?

..................................................................

4 What does your best friend usually wear?

..................................................................

5 Where do you buy your clothes?

..................................................................

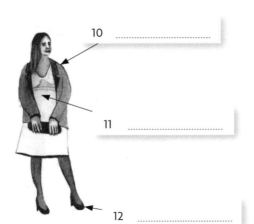

10 _____

11 _____

12 _____

**c** **Vocabulary bank** <u>Underline</u> the word that is different from the others.

1  hat         cap         <u>belt</u>
2  suit        boots       vest
3  wool        shorts      belt

4  sandals     boots       shorts
5  leather     suit        cotton

## 5 Pronunciation

**✱** /æ/ and /e/

**a** ▶**CD3 T37** Listen to the word pairs and repeat.

|   | /æ/ |   |   | /e/ |   |
|---|-----|---|---|-----|---|
| 1 | sad | ☐ | said | ☐ |
| 2 | bad | ☐ | bed | ☐ |
| 3 | man | ☐ | men | ☐ |
| 4 | dad | ☐ | dead | ☐ |
| 5 | sat | ☐ | set | ☐ |

**b** ▶**CD3 T38** Listen to the sentences. Tick (✔) the word you hear in the lists in Exercise 5a.

**c** ▶**CD3 T39** Now listen to these sentences and repeat.

1  Annie is Alan's best friend.
2  I'm helping Joanna in December and January.
3  Emma's jacket is black and yellow.
4  How many magazines is Danny sending?

## 6 Grammar

**✱** can/can't (asking for permission)

Write questions asking for permission. Then complete the answers with the words in the box.

They're really expensive.    I'm using it.    What's the problem?    Here you are.
~~What size?~~    We've got visitors.

1  try on / trainers?
A:  _Can I try on those trainers?_
B:  Yes, of course. _What size?_

2  borrow / dictionary?
A:  ......................................
B:  Sorry, not right now.

3  come round / your place?
A:  ......................................
B:  No, sorry. I'm busy.

4  see / homework?
A:  ......................................
B:  Yes, OK.

5  wear / sunglasses?
A:  ......................................
B:  No, you can't.

6  talk to you?
A:  ......................................
B:  Yes, of course.

## ✶ one/ones

**b** Complete the sentences with *one* or *ones*.

1 Mum, my jeans are really old. Can I have some new
   ....*ones*.... ?

2 Can I see the shirt in the window, please – the blue
   .................... ?

3 A: I love TV game shows.
   B: Me too! Which .................... is your favourite?

4 A: I like your ski jacket.
   B: Thanks. It's a new .................... . It's nice, isn't it?

5 A: I'd like two kilos of apples, please.
   B: Certainly. Would you like these green .................... ?
   A: No, the red .................... , please.

6 A: Those two people are from Russia.
   B: Which .................... ?
   A: The .................... in the corner, next to John and Linda.

## 7 Culture in mind

Match the words to make phrases. Then check with
the text on page 86 of the Student's Book.

1 capital ———— a dancing
2 film ————— b city
3 country        c Castle
4 army           d festival
5 guest          e band
6 Edinburgh      f houses

## 8 Study help

### ✶ Punctuation

**a** Which of these need a capital
letter at the beginning of the
word? Tick (✔) the boxes.

1 names of places    ✔
2 names of people    ☐
3 days of the week   ☐
4 months             ☐
5 seasons            ☐
6 colour adjectives  ☐
7 nationalities      ☐

**b** Which words need to start with
a capital letter? Correct them.

Britain      ....*Britain*....

friday       ....................

dave         ....................

autumn       ....................

japanese     ....................

yellow       ....................

august       ....................

spring       ....................

tuesday      ....................

april        ....................

To help you remember, you
can write the capital letter
in a different colour in your
Vocabulary notebook.

# Skills in mind

## 9 Listen

▶CD3 T40  Listen to Nadia talking to a woman in a clothes shop. Circle the correct answer: a, b or c.

| | | | | | | | |
|---|---|---|---|---|---|---|---|
| 1 | the thing Nadia wants | a | dress | b | shirt | c | jumper |
| 2 | colour | a | black | b | yellow | c | green |
| 3 | price | a | £54 | b | £45 | c | £49 |
| 4 | Nadia's size | a | 10 | b | 12 | c | 16 |
| 5 | the thing she tries on | a | top | b | trousers | c | jeans |

1 ........... blue ...........

## 10 Read

Read the text. Write words for colours in the pictures.

> **READING TIP**
>
> *Reading for specific information*
>
> Exercise 10 asks you to find information about the photos from the text.
>
> - There are four photos. Find the part of the text that tells you about each one.
> - Look for key words in the text. In this exercise, the key words are clothes and colours.

# Clothes in London

People in Britain wear all kinds of clothes – London is one of the world's centres for fashion. But some people wear special clothes when they are at work. Here are some examples.

In London you sometimes see British policemen with tall blue hats or helmets – they're the traditional British 'bobbies'. But these days, police officers in Britain usually wear black and white hats. They also wear black trousers and shoes, and white shirts.

In front of Buckingham Palace you can see the soldiers who guard the Palace and the Queen. They're called Coldstream Guards, and they wear their famous uniform of red jacket, black trousers and shoes, and a big black hat. (The hat is called a Busby.) The guards are also famous because they stand very still and never smile or talk!

In the business centre of London, you no longer see the traditional 'city gent' with his dark clothes and black bowler hat. Now, men who work in the city wear shirts and ties of different colours – but favourite colours are still grey or dark blue for trousers and jackets.

2 ........................................

3 ........................................

4 ........................................

5 ........................................

7 ........................................

6 ........................................

# Unit check

## 1 Fill in the spaces

Complete the sentences with the words in the box.

| at | in | festival | huge | clothes | enjoy | ~~party~~ | trousers | costume | parade |

I've got a photo here of me and my friends at Carlo's carnival _____party_____ . Everyone's wearing crazy
[1]_____ . Carlo's wearing a strange red [2]_____ , and Fiona has got short black [3]_____
and a [4]_____ hat. The carnival is [5]_____ April every year and it's a big [6]_____ in
my town. There's a [7]_____ in the streets – it starts [8]_____ 7 o'clock and lasts all evening.
We all really [9]_____ it.

☐ 9

## 2 Choose the correct answers

Circle the correct answer: a, b or c.

1 We don't wear scarves and _____ in hot
weather.
  a T-shirts   b jumpers   c jeans

2 He's wearing a white shirt and a black
_____ .
  a socks   b trousers   c hat

3 I wear _____ when I go running.
  a trainers   b dress   c shirt

4 The month after March is _____ .
  a February   b April   c June

5 _____ I look at your magazine, please?
  a Am   b Can   c Do

6 A: Which shoes do you like?
  B: I like the red _____ .
  a once   b one   c ones

7 Meet me _____ half past eleven.
  a at   b in   c on

8 _____ is my favourite season.
  a July   b Autumn   c August

9 A: I can't help you at the moment. Sorry.
  B: _____ .
  a Just a moment   b Here you are
  c Never mind

☐ 8

## 3 Vocabulary

Find eight more words for clothes in the
wordsnake. (There are three more words
which are not clothes.) Write the words on
the lines below.

dressbootsjacketscarfneckeyebeltsandalsshirttopsockshair

1 _____dress_____
2 _____
3 _____
4 _____
5 _____
6 _____
7 _____
8 _____
9 _____

☐ 8

## How did you do?

Total: ☐ 25

| 😊 Very good 20 – 25 | 😐 OK 14 – 19 | 🙁 Review Unit 11 again 0 – 13 |

# 12 He was only 22

## 1 Remember and check

Match the questions and answers about Buddy Holly. Then check on page 88 of the Student's Book.

1 Where was Buddy on 3 February 1959?
2 Who was with him?
3 Who were the three men?
4 What was the weather like?
5 How many people died in the plane crash?
6 How old was Richie Valens?

a They were singers and musicians.
b Seventeen.
c In a plane in Iowa, USA.
d Four.
e Richie Valens and the Big Bopper.
f It was very cold, with a lot of snow and wind.

## 2 Grammar

✱ Past simple: *was/wasn't*; *were/weren't*

**a** Complete the texts about these famous actors. Use *was* or *were*.

Marilyn Monroe [1] _____was_____ an American film star. Her real name [2] _____ Norma Jean Baker. She [3] _____ a beautiful woman and her films [4] _____ very popular. People all around the world [5] _____ very sad when she died in 1962.

Laurel and Hardy [6] _____ comedy actors. Stan Laurel [7] _____ from England. When he [8] _____ a teenager, he and Charlie Chaplin [9] _____ in the same English acting group. Oliver Hardy [10] _____ American. All their films together [11] _____ in black and white, and they [12] _____ very funny.

**b** Correct the statements about the people in Exercise 2a.

1 Marilyn Monroe was French.
   *No, she wasn't. She was American.*

2 She was a pop star.
   _____

3 People were happy when she died.
   _____

4 Laurel and Hardy's films were documentaries.
   _____

5 Laurel's first name was Oliver.
   _____

6 Their films were in colour.
   _____

**c** Look at the pictures and the times. Write past simple questions and short answers.

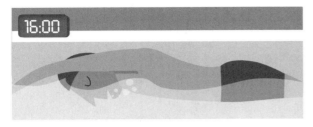

1   Joe / the station / 4 o'clock?

   A: *Was Joe at the station at 4 o'clock?*

   B: *No, he wasn't.*

2   Jane and Diana / the park / 2.30?

   A: ...........................................................

   B: ...........................................................

3   Julia / her bedroom / 9 o'clock?

   A: ...........................................................

   B: ...........................................................

4   Paul and Carol / the supermarket / 10.15?

   A: ...........................................................

   B: ...........................................................

5   Anna / the bookshop / 5.30?

   A: ...........................................................

   B: ...........................................................

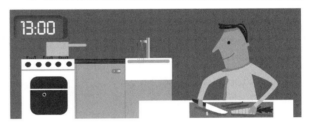

6   Matt / the kitchen / 1 o'clock?

   A: ...........................................................

   B: ...........................................................

# 3 Vocabulary

✳ Time expressions

**a** Complete the sentences with *last* or *yesterday*.

1   The bus was late <u>*yesterday*</u> afternoon.

2   My aunt and uncle were in Madrid .......................... week.

3   All my friends were at Karen's birthday party .......................... weekend.

4   The library wasn't open .......................... evening.

5   There was a good film on TV .......................... night.

6   We were late for school .......................... .

**b** Write true answers to these questions.

1   Where were you at 8.15 yesterday morning?

.........................................................................

2   Where were you at 5 pm last Friday?

.........................................................................

3   Were you in bed at 10 o'clock last night?

.........................................................................

4   Were you and your friends at school yesterday?

.........................................................................

5   Was your friend at your house last weekend?

.........................................................................

6   What day was your birthday last year?

.........................................................................

## 4 Remember and check

**CD3 T41** Complete this part of the conversation from Exercise 5 of the Student's Book. Use *was, wasn't, were* or *weren't*. Then listen and check.

**Alan:** What kind of music do you like, Gran?

**Gran:** Well my favourite group ¹ _were_ the Beatles.

**Alan:** Oh, right. ² _____ they from London?

**Gran:** No they ³ _____ ! They ⁴ _____ from Liverpool. Oh, they ⁵ _____ fantastic, just wonderful.

**Alan:** How many of them ⁶ _____ there – in the Beatles, I mean?

**Gran:** There ⁷ _____ four of them – John Lennon, Paul McCartney, George Harrison and Ringo Starr. They ⁸ _____ very young – and I ⁹ _____ very young too! John ¹⁰ _____ my favourite, but they ¹¹ _____ all great. All the girls in my school ¹² _____ crazy about them!

**Alan:** Right! Are their songs still on the radio?

**Gran:** Yes, they are. That song *Yesterday*, for example – that's a really famous Beatles song, they play that on the radio a lot.

## 5 Pronunciation

✱ *was/wasn't* and *were/weren't*

**a** **CD3 T42** Listen and repeat. <u>Underline</u> the words that are stressed.

| | |
|---|---|
| 1 Were they in <u>London</u>? | <u>Yes</u>, they <u>were</u>. |
| 2 Were they happy? | No, they weren't. |
| 3 Were the girls at home? | Yes, they were. |
| 4 Was he an actor? | Yes, he was. |
| 5 Was she worried? | No, she wasn't. |
| 6 Was Dave at school? | No, he wasn't. |

**b** **CD3 T43** <u>Underline</u> the words that you think are stressed. Then listen again, check and repeat.

1 Helen was in hospital on Wednesday.
2 Our parents were at the library yesterday.
3 When were you in Paris?
4 What was your address?

## 6 Vocabulary

✱ Ordinal numbers and dates

**a** Complete the table.

| | | | |
|---|---|---|---|
| 4 | Four | _4th_ | _fourth_ |
| 12 | Twelve | | |
| | | | second |
| | | | fifteenth |
| 3 | | | |
| 1 | | | |
| 50 | | 50th | |
| 22 | twenty-two | | |
| 31 | | | |

**b** Answer the questions.

1 What's the sixth month of the year?
   _June_

2 What's the ninth month?
   ...........................................

3 What's the last day of the school week?
   ...........................................

4 What's the second day of the weekend?
   ...........................................

5 What's your first lesson on Wednesday?
   ...........................................

**c** Write sentences with the dates as we say them.

1 Sheila's birthday / 17 May
   _Sheila's birthday is on the seventeenth of May._

2 Our national holiday / 3 July
   ...........................................

3 Christmas Day / 25 December
   ...........................................

4 New Year's Day / 1 January
   ...........................................

5 The festival / 9 October
   ...........................................

6 My party / 30 August / last year
   ...........................................

## 7 Everyday English

Complete the dialogues with the phrases in the box.

| Poor you!   my fault |
| you know    suddenly |

1 A: There was a problem with the electricity last night.
   B: I know. I was in my bedroom, and ........................... it was dark!

2 A: Where's Antonia?
   B: She's upstairs in the bathroom, ........................... , having a shower.

3 A: Look at the kitchen floor, Sophie! It's really dirty.
   B: Well, it isn't ........................... ! It was James – he was in the kitchen this afternoon.

4 A: I was in hospital yesterday. I had an accident.
   B: ........................... Are you OK now?

## 8 Study help

**★ Revision**

To revise words, it's a good idea to make vocabulary cards.

- Write a word on one side of the card and a translation or picture on the other side. Use the cards to test yourself, or ask another person to test you.

- Put vocabulary cards up around your room – on the walls, on the door, on your furniture. If you see the words often, they are easier to remember.

Think of some words that are important or difficult in Unit 12. Write them on these cards. Put the word on side A and the translation on side B.

Side A          Side B

_wallet_

# Skills in mind

## 9 Listen

**▶CD3 T44** Listen to the dates. Write the numbers 1–6.

a   03/03/2001   ☐     d   30/07/1995   ☐

b   25/11/1980   ☐     e   11/12/2004   1

c   31/08/1999   ☐     f   13/09/1959   ☐

## 10 Read

Read the text and answer the questions.

### Charlie Chaplin

Charlie Chaplin (1889–1977) was a very famous film star. He was from a poor home in South London, and he was already a comedy actor in the theatre when he was a teenager.

He went to the USA in 1910, and in 1914 he was in his first Hollywood film. In those days, the film industry was very young. Chaplin's early comedies were in black and white and they were 'silent' – there were no words or music.

Chaplin's favourite character was 'the tramp' – a little man with big trousers, an old black hat and a sad face. This was Chaplin's character in his famous comedy films – for example *The Kid* (1920), *The Gold Rush* (1924) and *City Lights* (1931). *Modern Times* (1936) was his first 'talking' film, and in *The Great Dictator* he was the director and music writer as well as the star.

Chaplin decided to leave the USA in 1952 and his new home was in Switzerland. He died there on Christmas Day at the age of 88.

1   What nationality was Charlie Chaplin?
*He was English.*

2   What city was he from?

3   When was he first in America?

4   Where was he in 1914?

5   Why were early films called 'silent films'?

6   When was *The Kid* first in the cinemas?

7   What was Chaplin's first film with words?

8   Where was Chaplin when he died?

> ### READING TIP
>
> *Answering questions*
>
> Make sure you know what the questions are asking. Study the question words.
>
> - If the question asks *When ...?*, the answer is a date or a time.
> - If it asks *Where ...?*, the answer is a place.
> - If it asks *Why ...?*, the answer is a reason (*Because ...*).

# Unit check

## 1 Fill in the spaces

Complete the sentences with the words in the box.

| was   were   wasn't   weren't   afternoon   ~~yesterday~~   fifth   way   first   recording |

Richard Deane is a piano player and a music teacher. At 10.00 _yesterday_ morning his [1]_____
music student was at the door, and there [2]_____ two others at 11.00 and 12.30. Richard
[3]_____ hungry, but there [4]_____ time for lunch – at 1.45 he was on his [5]_____
to North London in a taxi. At 2 o'clock in the [6]_____ he and his band were in the [7]_____
studio. But at the end of the day they [8]_____ very happy – their first four songs were OK,
but the [9]_____ one wasn't very good.

☐ 9

## 2 Choose the correct answers

(Circle) the correct answer: a, b or c.

1  22/05 is the _____ of May.
   a twenty-two   b (twenty-second)   c twentieth-two

2  Her birthday is _____ 16 March.
   a in   b on   c at

3  Kate was in Portugal _____ 2009.
   a in   b on   c at

4  Today is my father's _____ birthday.
   a forty   b fourteenth   c fortieth

5  Jack's cousins _____ in England last year.
   a are   b were   c was

6  I _____ angry with you last week.
   a wasn't   b were   c weren't

7  _____ there lots of children at the beach?
   a Is   b Were   c Was

8  Where _____ at 4 o'clock yesterday?
   a you were   b you was   c were you

9  I was ill _____ afternoon.
   a last   b yesterday   c before   ☐ 8

## 3 Vocabulary

Write the letters in the correct order to make words.

1  I was in Paris last *kewe*. _____week_____

2  My dad's birthday is the *driht* of November. _____

3  I wasn't well yesterday *oginmrn*. _____

4  My birthday is on the *venhtse* of April. _____

5  We always go on holiday in *stuAgu*. _____

6  I was at my friend's house yesterday *fonterano*. _____

7  I love *nuarJya* – in my country, it's a holiday! _____

8  Where were you last *thing*? _____

9  Today is the *wtntiteeh* of March. _____   ☐ 8

## How did you do?

Total: ☐ 25

| ☺ Very good 20 – 25 | ☺ OK 14 – 19 | ☹ Review Unit 12 again 0 – 13 |

# 13 What happened?

## 1 Remember and check

Complete the summary of the text about Rosa Parks. Use the adjectives in the box. Then check with the text on page 96 of the Student's Book.

angry   black   ~~full~~   little   tired   white   white

One day in December 1955, Rosa Parks got on a bus and sat down. Soon the bus was _____ full _____ .
The driver said to Rosa: 'Give this man your seat!'
Rosa was ¹ _____ , so she said: 'No.'
When Rosa was a ² _____ girl, she walked to school, but the ³ _____ children took a bus. Rosa went to a black school and studied with black children.

When Rosa said 'No' on the bus, she broke the law because a ⁴ _____ person had to give their seat to a ⁵ _____ person. The police took Rosa to prison. Black people in Alabama were
⁶ _____ , and they stopped using the buses. Then the law changed, and this changed the USA forever.

## 2 Grammar

### ✱ Past simple: regular verbs

**a** Complete the table.

| Verb | Past simple |
|------|-------------|
| 1  work | worked |
| 2  change | |
| 3  hate | |
| 4  study | |
| 5  die | |
| 6  stop | |
| 7  walk | |
| 8  start | |

**b** Complete the dialogues. Use five of the past simple verbs in Exercise 2a.

1   **Dad:**  Was the film good?
     **Tony:**  No. I _____ hated _____ it.

2   **Moni:**  Was Sarah angry?
     **Peter:**  Yes, she was. She _____ talking to me.

3   **Dave:**  Was Rosa Parks a teacher ?
     **Peggy:**  I don't think so. I think she _____ in a factory.

4   **Tom:**  What were you up to last night?
     **Fiona:**  Nothing much. I _____ for the English test at home.

5   **Lee:**  Were you on the school bus yesterday?
     **Chris:**  No, we _____ to school.

6   **Martin:**  Sandra looks sad. Do you know why?
     **Jane:**  Yes, her uncle _____ last week.

# 3 Pronunciation

**✱** *-ed* endings

| /t/ or /d/ | /ɪd/ |
|---|---|
| liked | hated |
| ................. | ................. |
| ................. | ................. |
| ................. | ................. |

**a** ▶CD3 T45 Write the verbs in the lists. Then listen and check.

~~liked~~ ~~hated~~ travelled called started landed watched wanted

**b** ▶CD3 T46 Listen and repeat. Make sure you say /ɪd/ for the *-ed* sound.

1 They visited a museum.
2 They landed on the moon.
3 The concert ended at 11 o'clock.
4 We waited at the station.

**c** ▶CD3 T47 Listen and repeat. Is the *-ed* sound /t/ or /d/? Write /t/ or /d/ in the spaces.

1 We watched a film. ....../t/......
2 He lived in Barcelona. .............
3 We helped Annie with her homework. .............
4 They laughed at me. .............
5 Sally stayed in a hotel. .............
6 We opened our books. .............

# 4 Grammar

**✱** Past simple: irregular verbs

**a** Fill in the crossword with the past simple forms of the verbs.

| Across | | Down | |
|---|---|---|---|
| 1 | leave | 2 | find |
| 3 | become | 3 | begin |
| 4 | eat | 6 | write |
| 5 | know | 8 | go |
| 7 | see | 10 | have |
| 9 | run | 12 | get |
| 11 | think | | |
| 13 | give | | |
| 14 | take | | |

Crossword: 1 across L E F T

**b** What did Angela do on Saturday morning? Look at the pictures and complete the paragraph.

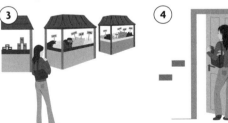

Angela ¹ ......*got up*...... at 8.30 and she ² ................. the dog for a walk. After breakfast she ³ ................. to the market. She ⁴ ................. home at 12.00 and then she ⁵ ................. to her friend Zoë. Angela and her family ⁶ ................. lunch at 1.15.

# 5 Grammar

### ✱ Past simple: questions and negatives

**a** Write positive and negative sentences. Use the past simple.

1 (stay) Last summer, Julia ___stayed in Paris___ .
_She didn't stay in Rome._

2 (play) Last night, Ben and Adam ___

3 (work) In 2002, Alan ___

Hi, Dad.

4 (phone) Yesterday, I ___

5 (dance / watch) On Friday, we ___

6 (park) On Saturday, Mum ___

**b** Put the verbs in brackets in the correct past simple form.

**Jason:** What ___did___ you ___do___ (do) last night?

**Sylvia:** We ¹___ (go) to the cinema. We ²___ (see) the new Spielberg film.

**Jason:** What time ³___ it ___ (begin)?

**Sylvia:** At 6.30.

**Jason:** Where ⁴___ you ___ (go) after the film?

**Sylvia:** To the Riverview Restaurant.

**Jason:** ⁵___ George ___ (have) dinner with you?

**Sylvia:** Yes, he did.

**Jason:** ⁶___ you ___ (sit) outside?

**Sylvia:** No, it was a bit cold, so we ⁷___ (sit) inside.

**Jason:** What ⁸___ you ___ (have) for dinner?

**Sylvia:** I ⁹___ (have) fresh fish with potatoes and salad.

**Jason:** Was it good?

**Sylvia:** Yes, it was delicious.

**Jason:** When ¹⁰___ you ___ (get) home?

**Sylvia:** At about 11.30.

# 6 Vocabulary

**★ Verb and noun pairs**

**a** Complete the sentences with the correct form of *have, play* or *go to*.

1   Kevin and Tony are ...*playing*... tennis this afternoon.

2   Do you want to _____ Eva's party?

3   My cousin _____ the piano.

4   Can I _____ an ice cream?

5   I like _____ lunch at this café.

6   We're _____ the cinema.

**b** **Vocabulary bank**   Write the words in the correct column.

> a break   a meal   ~~a noise~~   a photograph   a puzzle   an accident   fun   housework

| make | do | have | take |
|------|-----|------|------|
| *a noise* | | | |
| | | | |

# 7 Culture in mind

Match the two parts of the sentences. Check your answers with the text on page 100 of the Student's Book.

1   Elizabeth I was the daughter

2   She became queen

3   When she became queen, she was

4   She was educated and was

5   Elizabeth never

6   Elizabeth was queen of England

a   25 years old.

b   for 45 years.

c   of Henry VIII.

d   got married.

e   in 1558.

f   good at languages.

# 8 Study help

**★ Spelling and pronunciation**

**a** To remember the spelling rules for past simple verbs, you can group them like this in your Vocabulary notebook.

+ -ed
start – started
_____
_____

+ -d
love – loved
_____
_____

y + -ied
study – studied
_____

double letter
shop – shopped
_____

Add these words to the lists.

> marry   answer   dance   stop   play
> cry   travel   practise

**b** You can also group past simple verbs to show their pronunciation.

| /t/ | /d/ | /ɪd/ |
|-----|-----|------|
| helped | loved | started |
| | | |
| | | |
| | | |

Add the past simple form of these words to the lists.

> hate   travel   want   ask   enjoy
> watch   end   look   die

## 9 Listen

**▶ CD3 T48** Tony is on holiday in England with his father. Listen to his conversation with Sandro. Look at the pictures and ⟨circle⟩ the correct answer: A, B or C.

1 When did they arrive in London?

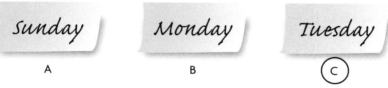

*Sunday*          *Monday*          *Tuesday*
   A                  B              Ⓒ

2 What time did the plane land?

   A                  B                 C

3 Where did they stay on Tuesday?

   A                  B                 C

4 What didn't they do in London?

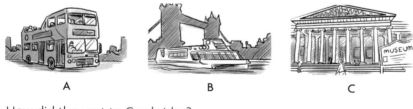

   A                  B                 C

5 How did they get to Cambridge?

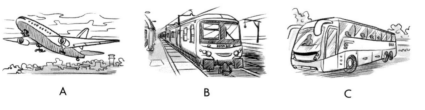

   A                  B                 C

**WRITING TIP**

*Writing an email to a friend*

- You can start with *Dear* (*Dear Carla*), but in emails people often say *Hi* (*Hi Carla*).

- Here are some endings you can use:
  *Love* (*from*)
  *Bye.*
  *See you soon.*
  *Write soon.*

## 10 Write

Write a reply to Carla's email. Tell her about the information you heard in Exercise 9.

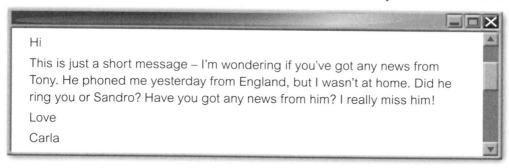

Hi

This is just a short message – I'm wondering if you've got any news from Tony. He phoned me yesterday from England, but I wasn't at home. Did he ring you or Sandro? Have you got any news from him? I really miss him!

Love

Carla

# Unit check

## 1 Fill in the spaces

Complete the sentences with the words in the box.

| were | on | didn't | in | ~~born~~ | stopped | studied | died | hospital | nurse |

My grandmother was ___*born*___ in Germany [1]_____ 18 February 1944. Her family moved to Italy [2]_____ 1960. She [3]_____ at the university in Milan and later she became a [4]_____ . She worked in a big [5]_____ in Bologna for four years, but after she was married she [6]_____ working. She and my grandfather had five children. They [7]_____ have a lot of money, but they [8]_____ very happy together. Grandma [9]_____ in 2008 – she was only 64. We still miss her a lot.

| 9 |

## 2 Choose the correct answers

(Circle) the correct answer: a, b or c.

1  I'd like to _____ an ice cream.
   a practise   b play   c (have)

2  Mum goes to _____ every morning.
   a work   b a bath   c a coffee

3  Andrew _____ the piano at the school concert.
   a had   b practised   c played

4  Men _____ on the moon in 1969.
   a landed   b ended   c started

5  Did she _____ a good time at the party?
   a has   b had   c have

6  The woman _____ open the door.
   a did   b didn't   c don't

7  What _____ last weekend?
   a you did   b do you did   c did you do

8  A: Did you talk to David yesterday?
   B: No, I _____ .
   a didn't   b doesn't   c don't

9  A: _____ did your cousins arrive?
   B: On Sunday.
   a Where   b When   c What

| 8 |

## 3 Vocabulary

(Circle) the correct answer: a, b or c.

1  My uncle _____ a bad accident last week.
   a (had)   b took   c did

2  My sister _____ a doctor in 2010.
   a become   b came   c became

3  Last weekend, we _____ to London.
   a go   b went   c gone

4  I _____ fifteen emails yesterday evening.
   a wrote   b writing   c written

5  My sister _____ my laptop, and she didn't ask me!
   a toke   b teak   c took

6  Oh – Canberra is the capital of Australia?
   I _____ it was Sydney.
   a think   b thank   c thought

7  Please don't _____ a lot of noise tonight.
   a make   b do   c have

8  I hate _____ housework!
   a doing   b making   c taking

9  Andy _____ some great photographs last week.
   a made   b took   c did

| 8 |

## How did you do?

Total: | 25 |

| 😊 | Very good 20 – 25 | 😐 | OK 14 – 19 | 😟 | Review Unit 13 again 0 – 13 |

# 14 Things change

## 1 Remember and check

**a** ▶ CD3 T49 Think back to the exercise with Dave (*D*) and his grandmother (*G*) on page 102 of the Student's Book. Match the two parts of the sentences. Then listen and check your answers.

1 G: When I was young, of course,
2 G: I think school life is more
3 G: I think people were
4 D: Some things now
5 D: I'm sure that now, life is
6 D: There are a lot more

a are difficult for my grandma.
b cars these days.
c difficult now, certainly.
d faster than in the 1960s.
e a lot of TV was in black and white!
f friendlier in the 60s than they are now.

**b** Find pairs of opposites in the box.

~~exciting~~ young crowded different
fast difficult empty happy slow
~~boring~~ sad easy the same old

_exciting_ _boring_
_____ _____
_____ _____
_____ _____
_____ _____
_____ _____

**b** Look at the picture and answer the questions. Write *A* or *B*.

1 Which dog is smaller? _B_
2 Which one is older? _____
3 Which one has got longer ears? _____
4 Which one has got curlier hair? _____
5 Which one is more excited? _____
6 Which one do you think is nicer? _____

## 2 Grammar

**✱ Comparison of adjectives**

**a** Complete the table.

| Adjective | Comparative adjective |
|-----------|----------------------|
| 1 hard | _harder_ |
| 2 hot | |
| 3 happy | |
| 4 difficult | |
| 5 unhappy | |
| 6 expensive | |
| 7 good | |
| 8 hungry | |
| 9 mysterious | |
| 10 bad | |

**c** Read the information about Brian and Rebecca, then complete the sentences. Use the comparative form of the adjectives in the box.

> bad   good   tall   interesting   ~~young~~   big

Rebecca                    Brian

|  | Rebecca | Brian |
|---|---|---|
| Age: | 16 | 15 |
| Height: | 1.7 m | 1.6 m |
| Brothers and sisters: | 4 | 1 |
| Maths results: | 75% | 70% |
| French results: | 38% | 41% |
| Art project: | | |

1 Brian is 15. He's ____younger____ than Rebecca.

2 Rebecca is 1.7 metres. She's _____ than Brian.

3 Rebecca's family is _____ than Brian's.

4 Rebecca's Maths results are _____ than Brian's.

5 But her French results are _____ than Brian's.

6 Brian's Art project is _____ than Rebecca's.

**d** Look at the pictures and write sentences. Use the comparative form of the adjectives in brackets.

1 (cold) *Today's colder than yesterday.*

2 (expensive) *The dress* _____

3 (interesting) _____

4 (busy) _____

5 (fast) _____

6 (good) _____

**e** Write true sentences comparing these things.

1 me – my best friend

........................................

........................................

........................................

2 my street – my friend's street

........................................

........................................

........................................

3 my town – (another place)

........................................

........................................

........................................

4 school days – weekends

........................................

........................................

........................................

5 comedy programmes – news programmes

........................................

........................................

........................................

6 History – English

........................................

........................................

........................................

# 3 Pronunciation

**✷ /ðən/ than**

▶CD3 T50 Listen to the sentences. <u>Underline</u> the words that are stressed. Listen again and repeat.

1 She's younger than him.
2 You're happier than me.
3 The bank is older than the bookshop.
4 Maths is more difficult than Science.
5 The book was more interesting than the film.
6 The shoes were more expensive than the trainers.

# 4 Vocabulary

**✷ Adjectives and opposites**

**a** Match the two parts of the sentences.

1 Some snakes               a   be quiet.
2 I didn't finish the book because it    b   look really old-fashioned now.
3 She couldn't sleep because the traffic    c   in a modern train.
4 We loved the film – it    d   was very noisy.
5 Don't climb on the roof – it    e   isn't safe.
6 You can travel very fast    f   are dangerous.
7 I'm watching this programme, so please    g   was boring.
8 Computers from the 1990s    h   was really exciting.

**b** Look at the pictures. Complete the sentences. Use six of the adjectives from Exercise 4a.

1 It was an ____*exciting*____ race.
2 A: Is this river _____ for swimming?
   B: No! There are alligators here!
3 A: What is it?
   B: It's an _____ washing machine.
4 They've got a _____ kitchen.
5 Don't go in there. It's _____ .
6 A: Oh! It's very _____ !
   B: What? I can't hear you.

**c** **Vocabulary bank** Write the opposite adjectives in the spaces.

a young man → an ¹ _____old_____ man

a friendly dog → an ² _____ dog

a ³ _____ window → a dirty window

a tidy room → an ⁴ _____ room

a comfortable armchair → an ⁵ _____ armchair

a light computer → a ⁶ _____ computer

a ⁷ _____ dinner → a heavy dinner

a light colour → a ⁸ _____ colour

## 5 Everyday English

Complete the dialogues. Use one word from Box A and Box B each time.

| A | B |
|---|---|
| What's   You   I don't   sort | of   believe it   the matter   see |

1  A: Did you like that programme on TV last night?

   B: Well, it was _____ interesting at first, but after twenty minutes I got bored.

2  A: You didn't come to my party on Saturday!

   B: I know. I'm sorry. _____ , my mother wasn't well so I stayed at home to help her.

3  A: _____ , Sandy?

   B: I got some really bad news. About my uncle in America.

4  A: Guess what? I asked Gloria to go to the cinema with me – and she said yes!

   B: _____ !

## 6 Study help

✳ Revision

When you're revising, try working with a friend. Make tests for each other. For example:

● Write sentences with a mistake in each one. Correct the mistakes in your friend's sentences. Here's one to practise. Can you see the mistake?

*My brother Ned is older then me.*

● Write sentences and leave empty spaces for one or two words. Fill in the words in your friend's sentences. Here's one to practise.

*Our cooker is _____ modern than our fridge.*

# Skills in mind

## 7 Listen

▶ **CD3 T51** Listen and write the names of the people and cats in the picture.

Tim ~~Frank~~ Anne Lisa Dad Uncle Bill Sandy Pablo

1 ..... *Frank* .....
2 .....................
3 .....................
4 .....................
5 .....................
6 .....................
7 .....................
8 .....................

### LISTENING TIP

*Revision*

For revision, use your Workbook recording. Practise the pronunciation exercises and listen to the dialogues.

- Play the recording often at home. For example, you can listen when you're getting dressed in the morning, or for ten minutes before you go to sleep.

- If possible, also play the recording when you're out. Listen on your way to school or when you're sitting in the bus.

## 8 Write

Write a paragraph comparing the two living rooms.

*Alan's room is smaller than Peggy's and it's got more modern furniture ...*

Alan's room

Peggy's room

# Unit check

## 1 Fill in the spaces

Complete the sentences with the words in the box.

> difficult    busier    ~~lived~~    more    modern    crowded    easier    was    town    old-fashioned

My family ___*lived*___ in the city for a long time, but in 1998 we moved to an old house in a small
¹_____ called Kingslea. Of course it ²_____ strange at first. London was a lot ³_____
and ⁴_____ exciting than Kingslea. We missed the ⁵_____ streets and the big shops. In our
house we had an ⁶_____ cooker so it was ⁷_____ to cook, and the toilet was at the end of
the garden. But later, when we got a ⁸_____ kitchen and bathroom, life was ⁹_____,
and now we love the place.

| 9 |

## 2 Choose the correct answers

Ⓒircle the correct answer: a, b or c.

1   Helen is taller _____ Wendy.
    a  that    b ⓣhan    c  then

2   This is a _____ road. There are lots of accidents
    here.
    a  quiet    b  safe    c  dangerous

3   That radio is 60 years old, so it's very _____ .
    a  funny    b  old-fashioned    c  noisy

4   Sorry, I can't talk to you now – I'm very _____ .
    a  busy    b  important    c  difficult

5   Joe is twelve, so he's _____ than William.
    a  younger    b  newer    c  more modern

6   This is terrible. The weather was awful yesterday
    and today it's _____ .
    a  bigger    b  better    c  worse

7   I was a _____ person before I came to this town.
    a  more happy    b  happier    c  happyer

8   My sister is taller than _____ .
    a  I    b  me    c  she

9   A:  Great! This T-shirt's only £3.50.
    B:  Yes, and the white one's _____ cheaper.
    a  lot    b  more    c  even

| 8 |

## 3 Vocabulary

Choose a word from the box to complete
each sentence. There are three words you
don't need.

> dirty    light    dark    heavy    old-fashioned
> difficult    quiet    safe    young    exciting
> big    ~~easy~~

1   I'm not worried about the test today – I'm
    sure it's very ___*easy*___ .

2   The football match yesterday was great – very,
    very _____ ! The score was 5–4!

3   That's a very _____ question. I don't
    know the answer.

4   Look at that telephone. It's from 1995! Wow,
    that's really _____ now.

5   Please be _____ , Mike. I'm talking to
    someone on the phone!

6   I'm not really hungry. Can I have a very
    _____ meal, please? Salad, perhaps?

7   Alex – can you clean the windows, please?
    They're _____ .

8   I'm sorry, I can't carry all these books. They're
    very _____ – about 10 kilos, I think!

9   Can you switch the lights on please? It's
    _____ in here! I can't read my book.

| 8 |

## How did you do?

Total: | 25 |

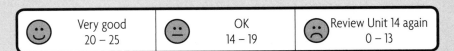

| 😊 | Very good 20 – 25 | 😐 | OK 14 – 19 | 🙁 | Review Unit 14 again 0 – 13 |

# Grammar reference

## Units 1 and 2

### The verb *be*: singular, plural, negatives and questions

1   We form the present simple of *be* like this:

| Singular | Plural |
|---|---|
| *I am* | *we are* |
| *you are* | *you are* |
| *he/she/it is* | *they are* |

2   In speaking and informal writing we use short forms.

   *I'm   you're   he's   she's   it's   we're   they're*

3   We use the verb *be* before a noun or an adjective.

   *He's an **actor**.   They're **footballers**.   I'm **American**.*

4   We make the negative by adding *not*.

   *I am **not**   you are **not***

   In speaking and informal writing we use short forms.

   *I'm **not**   you **aren't**   he **isn't**   she **isn't**   it **isn't**   we **aren't**   they **aren't***

5   To make questions we put the verb before the subject.

   ***Am I** right?*                *Yes, you **are**. / No, you **aren't**.*
   ***Are you** British?*        *Yes, I **am**. / No, I'm **not**.*
   ***Is he** an actor?*         *Yes, he **is**. / No, he **isn't**.*
   ***Is she** from Poland?*  *Yes, she **is**. / No, she **isn't**.*
   ***Are we** late?*             *Yes, we **are**. / No, we **aren't**.*
   ***Are they** singers?*      *Yes, they **are**. / No, they **aren't**.*

## Unit 1

### *wh-* question words

Questions with:

| | |
|---|---|
| *Who ...?* | ask about a person/people. |
| | ***Who** are they?   They're my friends.* |
| *What ...?* | ask about a thing/things. |
| | ***What**'s this?   It's a computer game.* |
| *When ...?* | ask about a time. |
| | ***When**'s the concert?   It's at seven o'clock.* |
| | ***When**'s your music lesson?   It's on Monday.* |
| *Where ...?* | ask about a place. |
| | ***Where**'s Moscow?   It's in Russia.* |
| *How old ...?* | ask about age. |
| | ***How old** are you?   I'm fifteen.* |
| *How many ...?* | ask about a number. |
| | ***How many** students are in your class?   Twenty-six.* |

## Unit 2

### Object pronouns

1   Here is a list of pronouns.

| Subject | *I* | *you* | *he* | *she* | *it* | *we* | *they* |
|---|---|---|---|---|---|---|---|
| Object | **me** | **you** | **him** | **her** | **it** | **us** | **them** |

2   We use object pronouns after the verb, instead of a noun.

*I like **the music**.*          *I like **it**.*
*I love **my mother**.*          *I love **her**.*
*They don't like **you and me**.*  *They don't like **us**.*
*I want to see **Jack and Sue**.*  *I want to see **them**.*

# Unit 3

## Present simple

1   We use the present simple for things that happen regularly or are normally true.

*We **watch** TV after school.*     *He **goes** shopping at the supermarket.*
*They **live** in Australia.*       *She **speaks** French.*

2   Usually the present simple is the same as the base form of the verb. But with a third person singular subject (*he, she, it*) we use an *s* ending.

*I **play** tennis.*                *She **plays** tennis.*
*My parents **work** in London.*    *My brother **works** in London.*

If a verb ends with *o, sh, ch, ss* or *x*, we add *es*.

*go – it goes    finish – he finishes    watch – she watches    miss – he misses    fix – she fixes*

If a verb ends with consonant + *y*, we change the *y* to *i* and add *es*.

*study – she studies    carry – he carries    fly – it flies*

3   We make the negative with *don't* (*do not*) or *doesn't* (*does not*) + base form of the verb.

*I **don't like** football.*        *He **doesn't like** football.*
*My cousins **don't live** in Italy.*  *Gina **doesn't live** in Italy.*

4   We make questions with *Do* or *Does* + base form of the verb.

***Do** you **like** me?*           ***Does** Helen **go** to school?*
***Do** we **know** the answer?*    ***Does** he **listen** to the radio?*
***Do** your parents **work**?*     ***Does** this shop **sell** chocolate?*

## Possessive 's

1   We put *'s* after a noun to say who something belongs to.

*Mum's car    John's family    Susan's bicycle*
*the dog's bed    my brother's problem    your sister's friend*

2   We <u>don't</u> usually say ~~the family of John~~, ~~the car of my father~~, etc.

## Possessive adjectives

1   Here is a list of possessive adjectives.

| Subject pronoun | *I* | *you* | *he* | *she* | *it* | *we* | *they* |
|---|---|---|---|---|---|---|---|
| Possessive adjective | ***my*** | ***your*** | ***his*** | ***her*** | ***its*** | ***our*** | ***their*** |

2   We use these adjectives before a noun to say who something belongs to.

***My** name's Steve.*              *I like **your** parents.*
*He's rich. Look at **his** car!*   *We love **our** dog.*
*She's a good teacher. We like **her** lessons.*  *They ride **their** bicycles to school.*
*The video isn't in **its** box.*

# Unit 4

## There's / there are

1   We use *there's / there are* to say that something exists.

***There's** a bank in South Street.*
***There are** two parks in my town.*  ***There are** lots of good restaurants here.*

2   The full form of *there's* is *there is*. In speaking and informal writing we usually say *there's*.

3   In positive sentences, we use *there's* + *a/an* + singular noun and *there are* + plural noun.
    **There's a** *parcel on the table.*
    **There's an** *interesting film on TV.*
    **There are** *good clothes at the market.*

4   In questions and negative sentences, we use *a/an* + singular noun and *any* + plural noun.
    **Is there** *a railway station here?*          **There isn't** *a railway station here.*
    **Are there** *any cafés in this street?*        **There aren't** *any cafés in this street.*

## Positive imperative

1   We use the imperative when we want to tell someone to do something.

2   The positive imperative is the same as the base form of the verb.
    **Turn** *left into Spring Street.*   **Sit** *down on that chair.*   **Be** *quiet, please!*

## Prepositions of place

We use prepositions of place to say where something or someone is.
*My pen is* **in** *my bag.*
*The box is* **on** *the table.*
*Our car is* **in front of** *the post office.*
*There's a garden* **behind** *the house.*
*There's a table* **next to** *my bed.*
*The bookshop is* **between** *the chemist and the newsagent.*

# Unit 5

## Why ...? because ...

*Why ...?* questions ask about the reason for something that happens. We usually answer the question with *because ...*
**Why** *do you want to see this band?*          **Because** *their music is fantastic.*

## has / have got

1   We use the verb *have got* to talk about things that people own.

2   Normally we use *have got*. But with a third person singular subject (*he, she, it*) we use *has got*. In speaking and informal writing we use the short forms *'ve* and *'s*.
    *I've* **got** *two brothers.*                 *Ben's* **got** *a new computer.*
    *They've* **got** *a DVD player.*              *My sister's* **got** *fair hair.*

3   The negative form is *haven't got / hasn't got*.
    *You* **haven't got** *a big family.*          *Alison* **hasn't got** *a mobile phone.*
    *We* **haven't got** *a computer at home.*     *My brother* **hasn't got** *fair hair.*

4   To make questions we use *Have/Has* + subject + *got*.
    **Have** *you* **got** *a bicycle?*            **Has** *she* **got** *blue eyes?*
    **Have** *we* **got** *a problem?*             **Has** *your uncle* **got** *a car?*

5   People sometimes use *have/has* without *got* – this is normal in the USA.
    *I* **have** *a bicycle.*       **Do** *we* **have** *a problem?*       *She* **doesn't have** *a mobile phone.*

# Unit 6

## Countable and uncountable nouns

1   Nouns in English are countable or uncountable. Countable nouns have a singular and a plural form.
    *apple – apples   tomato – tomatoes   book – books   question – questions   man – men*

2   Uncountable nouns don't have a plural form – they are always singular.
    *food   fruit   rice   bread   milk   music   money   hair   homework*
    *This* **food is** *delicious.*   *The* **music is** *awful!*   *Your* **hair is** *lovely.*   *My* **homework is** *in my bag.*

3   Some nouns can be countable or uncountable.
    *I want to buy two* **chickens** *at the market.*          (= *two whole birds, countable*)
    *Roast* **chicken** *is my favourite meal.*                (= *a type of meat, uncountable*)

4  With countable nouns, we can use *a/an* + singular noun and *some* + plural noun.
   *There's **a café** next to the cinema.*          *I'd like **some strawberries**.*
   *I often have **an egg** for breakfast.*          *There are **some** good **CDs** in that shop.*

5  With uncountable nouns, we use *some*.
   *I'm hungry. I want **some food**.*               *Please buy **some milk** at the supermarket.*

   We <u>don't</u> use *a/an* with uncountable nouns   ~~a bread~~   ~~an information~~

## this/that/these/those

1  We use *this* or *that* + singular noun. We use *these* or *those* + plural noun.
   **this** fruit   **that** book                    **these** clothes   **those** apples

2  We use *this* or *these* to point out things that are close to us. We use *that* or *those* to point out things that are at some distance from us.
   *Come and look at **this** letter.*               *Mmm! **These** strawberries are delicious.*
   ***That** man on the corner is our teacher.*      *Can you see **those** people over there?*

## I'd like … / Would you like …?

1  We use *would like* to ask for things or to offer things. *Would like* is more polite than *want*.
   *I'd **like** two kilos of apples, please.*       ***Would** you **like** vegetables with your meal?*

2  The full form of *I'd like* is *I would like*, but in speaking and informal writing we use the short form.

# Unit 7

## Adverbs of frequency

1  Adverbs of frequency are words that say how often we do things.
   *always   usually   often   sometimes   hardly ever   never*

2  Adverbs of frequency come <u>after</u> the verb *be*, but <u>before</u> other verbs.
   *I'm **usually** tired after school.*             *I **usually have** breakfast at 7.30.*
   *He's **always** late.*                           *She **always arrives** before me.*
   *We're **never** bored.*                          *We **never go** to that restaurant.*

# Unit 8

## Negative imperatives

We form the negative imperative with *Don't* + base form of the verb.
***Don't buy** those eggs – they aren't fresh.*   ***Don't cry** – it's OK.*   ***Don't be** stupid!*

# Unit 9

## can/can't (ability)

1  We use *can/can't* to talk about someone's ability to do something. The form is *can/can't* + base form of the verb.
   *I **can swim** 3 kilometres.*   *My little sister **can count** to 100.*   *We **can walk** on our hands.*
   *They **can't run** fast.*   *My father **can't ride** a horse.*   *We **can't speak** Chinese.*

2  To make questions we use *Can* + subject + base form of the verb.
   ***Can** your brother **swim**?*   ***Can** you **use** a computer?*   ***Can** they **play** the violin?*

   We <u>don't</u> use the verb *do* for questions or negatives.

## like / don't like + -ing

1  We often use the *-ing* form of a verb after *like, enjoy, love* and *hate*.
   *He likes cycling.*   *I love swimming.*   *They enjoy watching tennis.*
   *Anne doesn't like skiing.*   *She hates playing computer games.*

2  If a verb ends in *e*, we drop the *e* before adding *ing*.
   *live – living   ride – riding*

If a short verb ends in 1 vowel + 1 consonant, we double the final consonant before adding *ing*. We do the same if the verb ends in 1 vowel + l.

*get – get**ting**   shop – shop**ping**   swim – swim**ming**   travel – travel**ling***

# Unit 10

## Present continuous

1   We use the present continuous to talk about things happening at the moment of speaking.
     *The girls **are doing** their homework now.*
     *Alex is in the bathroom. He**'s having** a shower.*
     *Don't make a noise. I**'m listening** to the radio.*

2   We form the present continuous with the present simple of *be* + *-ing* form of the verb.
     *I**'m having** lunch.*                          *You**'re shouting**!*
     *He**'s playing** volleyball.*                   *We**'re sitting** in the garden.*
     *It**'s raining**.*                              *They**'re studying** in the library.*

3   We make questions and negatives with the question/negative form of *be* + *-ing* form of the verb.
     *I**'m not watching** TV.*                       ***Are** you **speaking** to me?*
     *You **aren't listening** to me!*                ***Is** he **doing** his homework?*
     *She **isn't playing** well today.*              ***Are** they **travelling** in France?*

4   Some verbs aren't normally used in the present continuous, for example:
     *understand   know   like   hate   remember   forget   want*

5   Look at the difference between the present continuous and the present simple.
     *I usually **do** my homework in my bedroom, but today I**'m doing** it in the dining room.*
     *My father hardly ever **watches** TV, but this afternoon he**'s watching** the football.*
     *I **listen** to music every day. At the moment, I**'m listening** to the new Lady Gaga album.*

# Unit 11

## Prepositions of time: *at, in, on*

1   We use *at* with times, and with the word *night*.
     *The lesson starts **at nine o'clock**.*
     *I get up **at 6.30**.*
     *My uncle works **at night**.*

2   We use *in* with parts of the day (but not with *night*), and with months and seasons.
     *I go to school **in the morning**.*             *I often read **in the evening**.*
     *Her birthday is **in September**.*              *We go on holiday **in August**.*
     *It's always cold **in winter**.*               *I like going to the beach **in summer**.*

3   We use *on* with days of the week.
     *We have an English lesson **on Monday**.*       *I usually go to the cinema **on Saturday**.*

## Asking for permission: *Can I ...? / Yes, you can. / Sorry, you can't.*

1   We often use *Can I ...?* to ask for permission to do something.
     ***Can I** leave now, please?*    ***Can I** go to the party on Saturday?*

2   To give or refuse permission we use *can* or *can't*.
     ***Can I** borrow your jacket?*
     *Yes, you **can**.    No, sorry, you **can't**. I want to wear it tonight.*

## *one/ones*

We use *one* or *ones* when we don't want to repeat a noun. We use *one* instead of a singular noun and *ones* instead of a plural noun.

*My bicycle's very old. I want a new **one**. (= bicycle)*
*I've got a CD by Britney Spears, but it's an old **one**. (= CD)*
*I'd like two chocolate ice creams and two strawberry **ones**. (= ice creams)*
*Do you know those boys – the **ones** in the café? (= boys)*

# Unit 12

## Past simple: *was/wasn't; were/weren't*

1   We use the past simple form of *be* to talk about actions and events in the past.

2   We form the past simple like this:

*I was*                            *we were*
*he/she/it was*                    *you were*
                                   *they were*

*I was in town on Saturday.*       *He was tired after the match.*       *It was hot last week.*
*You were late yesterday.*         *We were at the cinema last night.*   *They were angry.*

3   We make the negative by adding *not* (*was not, were not*). In speaking and informal writing we use short forms: *wasn't* and *weren't*.

*I wasn't here last year.*         *The film wasn't interesting.*
*You weren't at school yesterday.* *They weren't at the concert.*

4   To make questions we put the verb before the subject.

*Were you in town on Saturday?*    *Was James happy about the test?*

5   We often use time expressions with the past simple.

*yesterday    yesterday morning    yesterday afternoon    yesterday evening*
*last night    last Friday    last week    last weekend    last month    last year*

# Unit 13

## Past simple – regular verbs

1   We use the past simple to talk about actions and events in the past.

2   With regular verbs we form the past simple by adding *ed*. The form is the same for all subjects.

*I walked to school yesterday.*    *She opened the door.*              *The concert started at 8 o'clock.*
*You finished before me.*          *We played cards last night.*       *They watched the news on TV.*

3   If a verb ends with consonant + *y*, we change the *y* to *i* and add *ed*.

*study – studied    marry – married    carry – carried*

If a short verb ends in 1 vowel + 1 consonant, we double the final consonant before adding *ed*. We do the same if the verb ends in 1 vowel + *l*.

*stop – stopped    hop – hopped    travel – travelled*

4   We make the negative with *didn't* (*did not*) + base form of the verb.

*I didn't walk to school yesterday.*   *She didn't open the door.*
*You didn't finish before me.*         *We didn't play cards last night.*

5   We make questions with *Did* + subject + base form of the verb.

*Did I start before you?*          *Did he open the window?*
*Did you walk to school yesterday?*  *Did they play volleyball last week?*

## Past simple – irregular verbs

1   A lot of common verbs are irregular. This means that the past simple forms are different – they don't have the usual *ed* ending.

*go – went    see – saw    find – found    write – wrote    think – thought*

There is a list of irregular verbs on page 127 of the Student's Book.

2   We make questions and negatives in the same way as for regular verbs.

*I went to town, but I didn't go to the bookshop.*   *Did you go to the newsagent?*
*We saw James, but we didn't see Jonathan.*           *Did you see Alison?*

# Unit 14

## Comparison of adjectives

1 To compare two things, or two groups of things, we use a comparative form + *than*.
   *I'm **older than** my brother.*
   *France is **bigger than** Britain.*
   *TVs are **more expensive than** radios.*
   *Your computer is **better than** mine.*

2 With short adjectives, we normally add *er*.
   *old – old**er**   cheap – cheap**er**   quiet – quiet**er***

   If the adjective ends in *e*, we add only *r*.
   *nice – nice**r**   safe – safe**r**   free – free**r***

   If the adjective ends with consonant + *y*, we change the *y* to *i* and add *er*.
   *easy – eas**ier**   early – earl**ier**   happy – happ**ier***

   If the adjective ends in 1 vowel + 1 consonant, we double the final consonant and add *er*.
   *big – big**ger**   sad – sad**der**   thin – thin**ner***

3 With longer adjectives, we don't change the adjective – we put *more* in front of it.
   *expensive – **more** expensive   difficult – **more** difficult   interesting – **more** interesting*

4 Some adjectives are irregular – they have a different comparative form.
   *good – **better**   bad – **worse***